Also by Hugh Carpenter and Teri Sandison

Fast Entrées
Wok Fast
Fast Appetizers
Hot Chicken
Hot Pasta
Hot Barbecue
Hot Vegetables
Hot Wok
The Great Ribs Book

Fast Fish

Hugh Carpenter
and Teri Sandison

TEN SPEED PRESS
Berkeley | Toronto

Ten Speed Press
PO Box 7123
Berkeley, California 94707
www.tenspeed.com

Distributed in Australia by Simon & Schuster Australia, in Canada by Ten Speed Press Canada,
in New Zealand by Southern Publishers Group, in South Africa by Real Books, and in the
United Kingdom and Europe by Airlift Book Company.

Cover and text design by Beverly Wilson
Typography by Laurie Harty

Library of Congress Cataloging-in-Publication Data

Carpenter, Hugh.
Fast fish / Hugh Carpenter and Teri Sandison.
        p. cm.
Summary: "The fourth book in the Fast series, featuring buying, storage, and cooking tips for fish,
along with more than 100 easy recipes for black cod (sablefish), catfish, halibut, salmon, snapper,
sole, swordfish, trout, and tuna"--Provided by publisher.
Includes index.
ISBN-10: 1-58008-648-9 (pbk.)
ISBN-13: 978-1-58008-648-6
1. Cookery (Fish). 2. Quick and easy cookery. I. Sandison, Teri. II. Title.
TX747.C3375 2005
641.6'92--dc22   2004022455

Printed in China
First printing, 2005

1 2 3 4 5 6 7 8 9 10 — 09 08 07 06 05

This book is lovingly dedicated to

Alex Levin and Susan Vogt

1941–2003.

Teachers, parents, lovers of life—

they lit the path

so the rest of us could see.

Contents

Introduction 8

Fish Tips 10

Cooking Techniques 13

Essential Equipment 18

Essential Pantry 20

Black Cod (Sablefish) 24

Catfish 34

Halibut 42

Salmon 54

Snapper 70

Sole 78

Swordfish 84

Trout 92

Tuna 98

Tartar Sauces, Salsas, and Relishes 106

Acknowledgments 109

Artist Credits 109

Index 110

Introduction

Perfectly cooked fresh fish is a true taste sensation. With its slight firmness and subtle, sweet taste, fish is as nicely accented by a squeeze of lemon or a spoonful of tartar sauce as by a more complex salsa or sauce.

This book teaches you how to select the freshest fish, how to store it, and how to determine when it is perfectly cooked. It also offers 100 simple, flavor-intense recipes that will turn even the fish skeptic into a fish lover.

Fresh fish is fragile, it overcooks quickly, and it demands supervision. That is why we usually cook fish for work-night meals and accompany it with uncomplicated side dishes. Examples of easy accompaniments are lightly charred flour tortillas, steamed rice, rice pilaf, roasted fingerling potatoes, hot dinner rolls, or garlic bread. You could also do a quick-to-make salad or vegetable dish. By keeping the dinner menu straightforward, there are no distractions from the central fish entrée.

Fish consumption is on the rise, possibly because of its widely acknowledged health benefits—it is rich in omega-3 fatty acids and low in fat. Eating fish has been linked to alleviating depression, possibly preventing Type 2 diabetes, and lowering the risks of heart disease and cancer. According to the U.S. Commerce Department's National Oceanic and Atmospheric Administration, Americans ate a record 16.3 pounds of fish and shellfish per person in 2003, up from 15.6 pounds in 2002. The 2003 figure represents a 4 percent increase. Over the last thirty years, fish consumption, both for dine-out and retail sales, has shown a steady increase. Upscale markets offer increasing varieties of fish, beautifully displayed and sold by knowledgeable staff. At the same time, supermarket chains are moving toward prepackaged, case-ready fish with extended shelf life improved by new, modified-atmosphere packaging. Visit any market and you'll be likely to find farm-raised striped bass, sturgeon, and walleyed pike, in addition to farm-raised salmon, catfish, and trout.

Along with the positive aspects of the wider availability of fresh fish, there are also cautions to heed. The purity of all of our foods is in various stages of being compromised. In the case of some fish, this is reflected by reports showing contamination by mercury and other toxins. Mercury tends to accumulate in the food chain: the higher on the chain, the greater the concentration of mercury. But species rich in omega-3 fats also tend to be the food chain's higher-ups, and they include swordfish, mackerel, and tuna (but so far salmon has tested very low for mercury). Putting the concerns about trace elements and toxins into perspective, the American Heart Association, in November 2002, re-emphasized its recommendation that adults eat at least two servings of fish per week.

Environmental issues concerning fish are in constant flux. A species of fish endangered a few years ago may be more plentiful today. A previously pristine ocean area may now be degraded by industrial pollution. Commercial salmon farmers are rushing to modify farming practices in response to public criticism about feeding methods. It's the responsibility of each of us to be better informed and to demand complete information from food experts, food retailers, and our government.

How to Use This Book
This book focuses on the nine most popular fish sold in the United States. But there are dozens of other wonderful fish available. At the beginning of each chapter you'll find a list of other varieties of fish that can be substituted.

You'll notice throughout this book our rules for fish: buy fresh, lower the heat rather than raise it, and err on the side of undercooking (fish can always be returned to the broiler, barbecue, or pan). Most of the recipes serve four, but any of them can be cut in half or doubled.

If you are not entirely confident about cooking a particular fish, review the chapter introduction first. It will only take a few minutes, and the information can be surprisingly helpful. The section about cooking techniques (page 13) provides the foundation for the recipes, and we refer to this often throughout the book. Essential Equipment (page 18) surveys everything necessary for cooking fish as well as gadgets that make recipe preparation quicker. And the Essential Pantry (page 20) reviews specialty items and the brands that are the flavor foundations for the recipes.

Once you choose a recipe, read through the directions. Be sure to complete all of the preparation steps included in the ingredient list (such as mincing garlic or making a salsa featured in another chapter of the book); the recipe directions assume you have completed these steps.

Hugh Carpenter and Teri Sandison

Fish Tips

Choosing Fish

Because we live close to the California coast, we always buy fresh fish. But it's not true that "fresh" fish is always better than frozen fish. Deep-sea fishing boats can hold fish at just above the freezing point for two weeks before the fish is brought to shore and sent to market as "fresh fish." New super-freezing techniques that freeze fish at 76 degrees below zero can make it virtually impossible to tell frozen from fresh. Are you aware, for example, that 50 to 60 percent of all sushi-grade fish in the United States is frozen at some point in its journey from the ocean to the sushi counter?

Improper freezing is what gives frozen fish its bad reputation. Problems include poor freezing techniques, or thawing and refreezing the fish at the processing plant. The higher the fat content, the less adversely the fish is affected by freezing. Fish that are the least affected by freezing are tuna, black cod (sablefish), arctic char, and Chilean sea bass.

Once you know how to identify perfect fish, you'll never have to ask the fish expert what fish is the freshest. Perfect fish, whether whole or cut into steaks or fillets, *glistens*; it has a glossy sheen on the surface. This gloss is caused by a layer of mucus that protects the flesh. The layer of moisture evaporates with time, and the gloss dulls to a brown, milky appearance.

Go to the best fish market or supermarket in your area. Notice the difference in sheen, glossiness, and color between fresh fish and fish that has been in the fish case for a few days. With fresh fish the light seems to reflect and bounce as you view the fish from different angles. The flesh appears tightly connected, with no areas of separation, and there is no liquid around the fish.

Perfect fish cut into fillets and steaks has no odor. If the fish has not been prepackaged, ask your fish seller to let you examine the fish more closely. *If it doesn't have a glossy sheen and has any odor, don't buy it*. If the fish is whole, it should have clear eyes, bright red gills, firm flesh, and tightly adhering scales.

FOR MORE INFORMATION

We suggest you monitor the ever-changing world of fish by consulting the following websites:

www.mbayaq.org

www.noaa.gov/fisheries.html

www.seafoodchoices.org

Freezing and Thawing Fish

We're opposed to freezing fresh fish at home. The home freezing process isn't quick enough and home freezers are not sufficiently cold to prevent the texture of the fish from being compromised. Fish frozen at home and then defrosted will always taste inferior to flawlessly fresh fish or fish that has been commercially frozen and properly thawed by the market.

Frozen fish should be thawed overnight or throughout the day in the refrigerator. The slower fish is thawed, the less adversely it is affected by the freezing process. Never try to speed the process by thawing fish in the microwave, in cold water, or on the kitchen counter. The texture will be badly compromised and the fish will be a taste flop!

Storing Fish

Store fresh fish in the coldest environment possible without freezing. Ask the market to place a bag of crushed ice next to the package of fish so that it doesn't warm during the trip home. Once at home, refrigerate the fish immediately. If you are cooking the fish that day, keep it in its wrapping.

If the fish isn't going to be cooked the day of purchase, remove the fish from its package and wrap in plastic wrap. Cover the fish with a bag of ice and refrigerate. The surface of the fish next to the ice will not freeze; rather, because cold air descends, the layer of ice will cause the entire piece of fish to be much colder than any of the surrounding foods in the refrigerator and it will stay fresher longer.

If you live on the coast, always cook fish **within three days of purchase.** If you live away from the coast, always cook the fish **within two days of purchase.** It may not have begun to smell, but it is not perfect fish. At the end of this time period, if you decide to go out to dinner or to cook something else, cook the fish anyway. Just rub it with oil, salt, and pepper, and microwave, broil, or barbecue it. Refrigerated, the cooked fish will stay in flawless condition for three additional days. Use it for a cold entrée, break it into small pieces for salads, or slice it thinly to make fish sandwiches.

Rinsing Fish

Among the experts, there is no agreement on whether or not fish should be rinsed prior to preparation. Most food scientists feel that fish should be given a brief rinsing. Along with most chefs, I prefer not to rinse fresh fish fillets and steaks. Fresh fish is absorbent. When rinsed, it will absorb some of the water. Then, when marinated, the fish will absorb less marinade because it is already saturated with liquid. This is particularly true for flaky fish such as salmon, halibut, and sea bass.

But doesn't washing fish make it "safer" to eat? No. Bacteria that *may* be present on fish is colorless and odorless. Rinsing fish does not remove all the bacteria; they are killed during proper cooking. The bottom line: if the fish looks as if it should be rinsed, it shouldn't be bought.

Marinating Fish

Marinating fish before cooking accents its subtle flavors. A marinade can be as simple as rubbing the fish with extra virgin olive oil, salt, pepper, and a squeeze of lemon or using an oil and vinegar salad dressing.

Fish varies in its ability to absorb marinade. Flaky fish (salmon, halibut, sea bass, and cod, for example) absorb a marinade within a matter of minutes. Firm fish (swordfish, tuna, and shark, for example) have a dense texture; the marinade will penetrate only slightly into the fish.

Marinate all fish for five to fifteen minutes—no longer—and always in the refrigerator. If the marinade has salt, longer marinating will extract moisture from the fish and cause the texture to become spongy. If the marinade contains an acid such as lemon juice, longer marinating will "cook" the surface of the fish.

Marinating fish for hours in a salty or high acid mixture is an essential technique when creating raw fish dishes such as gravlox and ceviche. However, these recipes are not fast and thus do not appear in this cookbook.

Flouring or Battering Fish

Battering fish is most commonly done when pan-frying. Coating the fish with flour or a batter protects the fragile flesh from drying, turns the surface a beautiful golden color, and gives the exterior a pleasing crunch.

For a thin protective layer for pan-frying: Moments before cooking, coat the fish with flour, cornstarch, or dried powdered bread crumbs, shaking off all excess. You can dust the fish on a plate, on paper towels, or inside a resealable plastic bag. Immediately place the fish in the preheated pan.

For a thick protective coating for pan-frying, deep-frying, or roasting: Dust the fish with white flour, shaking off the excess. Dip the fish in beaten egg. Turn the fish over on a plate of dried bread crumbs or ground nuts, coating evenly. Transfer the fish to a wire rack. Cook the fish immediately or refrigerate and cook up to 6 hours later.

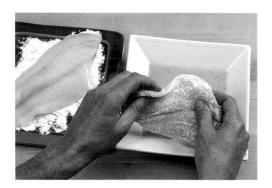

Determining Doneness

Most fish is perfectly cooked when the interior loses its opaque or raw coloring. Tuna is an exception, since it should always be served with an interior that ranges from raw to medium rare. Some cooks prefer slightly undercooked fish so that the thickest part of the fish has not quite lost its opaque coloring. This is a matter of personal preference.

Use one or a combination of any of the following techniques for determining doneness. When in doubt, err on the side of undercooking fish. If the fish is not fully cooked, it can always be returned to the barbecue, broiler, microwave, or sauté pan. Overcooked fish is a taste disaster.

Using a knife and fork, try separating the flesh. The moment the fish begins to flake when prodded with a fork, it's done.

Using the blunt end of a bamboo chopstick, gently push on the fish. The fish is perfectly cooked when the chopstick sinks easily into the interior of the fish.

Insert an instant-read meat thermometer into the deepest part of the fish. Cook the fish to 135°F for slightly undercooked and 140°F for fully cooked.

Use the Perfect Fish Cooking Timer, a calibrated measurer made by SCI. This gadget estimates the cooking time based on the thickness of the fish.

Use the Grill Per'fect by Burton. Inserted into the fish, this handy device changes color when the fish is perfectly cooked.

WHY FISH SMELLS DURING COOKING

Perfectly fresh fish never has an odor. But one cooking technique, pan-frying, causes even the freshest fish to release a characteristic fish smell (albeit one that is very different from the odor of spoiling fish). This is caused by the contact of hot fat with the surface of the fish in an open pan. If you dislike this smell, choose another cooking technique such as roasting, broiling, steaming, microwaving, or barbecuing.

Cooking Techniques

"Flaky" or "firm" is a useful way to categorize fish and these terms help determine the cooking technique. The barbecue technique, for example, differs radically depending on whether the fish is firm or flaky. A lowfat firm fish such as swordfish quickly loses its moist interior even when slightly overcooked, while a less firm, higher fat fish such as salmon or black cod (sablefish) can be overcooked and still be moist. If you are new to fish cooking, choose a flaky fish with a high fat content; the results are more dependable.

Flaky fish has a rather loosely knit grain structure, which often appears in a herringbone pattern. When bent slightly, the flesh will begin to tear. **Examples of flaky fish, listed in order of fat content, are:** American sole, petrale sole, freshwater bass, sea trout, bluefish, butterfish, Atlantic croaker, black sea bass, pike, pollack, rockfish, snapper, lemon sole, catfish, walleyed pike, tilapia, trout, black cod (sablefish), grouper, halibut, monkfish, orange roughy, striped bass, Atlantic salmon, arctic char, Chilean sea bass, coho salmon, sockeye salmon, king salmon.

Firm fish, by contrast, has a densely structured grain. When fish fillets or steaks are gently bent, the flesh stays tightly bound together. Firm fish feels dense and heavy compared to flaky fish. **Examples of firm fish, listed in order of fat content, are:** cordova, mahi mahi, bigeye tuna, black drum, lingcod, yellowfin tuna, shark, swordfish, ono, opah, bluefin tuna, sturgeon, yellowtail.

Barbecuing

Barbecuing is the easiest way to create complex-tasting fish entrées with a minimum of preparation time.

To add an intense additional flavor, soak 2 cups of wood chips, such as hickory, pecan, and apple wood, in cold water for 30 minutes. Just before cooking, drain the chips. For gas grills, place the chips on a layer of aluminum foil positioned at one corner of the cooking grate or inside the wood chip smoker tray. For charcoal grills, scatter the wet wood chips directly on the coals just before barbecuing the fish.

Barbecuing Flaky Fish
(see list at left)

Method #1: Prepare a medium-hot fire in a charcoal grill or preheat a gas grill to medium (about 450°F). Lay the fish skin side down on the grill rack. If the fish is skinned, place it on a layer of oiled aluminum foil or on a tight layer of thinly sliced citrus (lemons, limes, oranges, or grapefruit). The fish skin or the layer of citrus will not burn away.

The moment the fish is placed in the barbecue, close the lid. No peeking—the lid should remain closed throughout cooking. Fish that is ½ inch thick should be checked after 6 minutes; fish that is 1 inch thick should be checked after 10 minutes. Lift the lid and check for doneness as described on page 12. If the fish is not ready, close the lid and cook for 1 to 2 minutes, then remove the lid and check again. Repeat this covering/uncovering process to check doneness until the fish is perfectly cooked.

Slide an offset spatula between the fish and its skin (or the foil or layer of citrus) and transfer to dinner plates or a serving platter.

Method #2: Prepare a medium-hot fire in a charcoal grill or preheat a gas grill to medium (about 450°F). Place the fish in a fish grill screen (see page 18) that has been coated with nonstick spray or rubbed with oil. If the fish screen has a detachable handle, cover the barbecue and cook the fish over medium heat. If the fish screen doesn't have a detachable handle, close the lid as much as you can, and cook over medium heat. Cook, turning several times, until the fish is done.

Barbecuing Firm Fish

(see list on page 13)

Grilling firm fish requires a temperature gauge in the barbecue lid so that the temperature can be accurately controlled. If the lid doesn't have a temperature gauge, insert a long-stemmed oven thermometer through a vent on a charcoal grill lid, or into a hole drilled in the lid of your gas grill.

Prepare a medium-hot fire in a charcoal grill or preheat a gas grill to medium (about 450°F). Brush the grill rack with vegetable oil. Immediately place the fish directly on the rack. The fish should make a sizzling noise. If it does not, remove the fish and increase the heat, then return the fish to the rack.

Whether using a charcoal or gas grill, the first step is to mark the fish. Cook, turning once, for about 2 minutes on each side, until the fish turns a light golden and picks up the pattern of the barbecue grate.

For charcoal grills, temporarily remove the grate holding the fish from the barbecue. Push the charcoal to one side, or push the coals into a thin layer around the entire outside area of the barbecue. Immediately return the grate holding the fish to the barbecue. Cover the barbecue with its lid. Adjust the bottom and top vents so that the heat is always maintained in the 300°F to 325°F range.

For gas grills, turn all of the burners to the lowest setting. Cover the grill and keep the heat set at about 300°F. If the heat goes above 325°F, turn off one of the burners. If still too hot, turn off all but one of the burners and move the fish as far from the heat source as possible. If the heat is still above 325°F, prop the lid open with tongs so that some of the heat is flushed out of the barbecue.

On both charcoal and gas grills, remove the lid every 1 to 2 minutes. Baste the fish, turn over, baste again, and then cover the barbecue. Repeat the process until the fish is cooked (see page 12). Transfer to a serving platter or plates and serve at once.

Barbecuing-Roasting

In adverse weather or when you don't want to spend as much time supervising the fish during barbecuing, you can combine barbecuing and roasting.

Prepare a medium-hot fire in a charcoal grill or preheat a gas grill to medium (about 450°F). Preheat the oven to 300°F.

Grill the fish, turning once, for about 2 minutes on each side, until lightly golden (you'll need to barbecue flaky fish in a fish grill screen). Transfer the fish to a wire rack placed on a baking sheet and finish cooking the fish in a 300°F oven. The fish will taste as if it has been cooked entirely on the barbecue.

Broiling

Broiling fish is a quick cooking method, but it's necessary to continually monitor what's going on in the oven. You often need to combine broiling with low-temperature roasting to ensure that the fish doesn't get overdone. Cooked this way, the fish never scorches, nor does it need to be turned over or lowered to another oven rack. For this method, limit the thickness of the fish to 1½ inches or less.

Place the marinated fish in a single layer in a heavy baking dish that has been lined with aluminum foil.

Position a rack 4 inches from the heating element and turn the oven to broil. Immediately place the baking dish on the rack and close the oven door. That's right—the oven is not preheated.

Broil the fish for 5 to 8 minutes, until it is light golden on top. Check to see if the fish is fully cooked (see page 12). If the fish is not fully cooked, turn the oven to bake at 300°F and continue cooking the fish until done. Transfer to a serving platter or dinner plates and serve.

Roasting

Roasting fish is a simple cooking technique that necessitates little attention. It allows you free time to complete the accompanying dishes. Unlike baking, roasting is done in an open container.

Choose a heavy roasting or baking dish so that it doesn't buckle during cooking. To minimize cleaning chores, line the dish with aluminum foil.

Nearly all roasting recipes in this book use a 400°F to 450°F oven. The high heat colors the top surface of the fish and cooks the flesh quickly without drying it out. If the oven has the convection feature, the cooking time will be about 15 percent shorter.

Sometimes salmon and halibut fillets are roasted at 300°F. The fish will be wonderfully moist with a nice pink or white color. Other fish aren't cooked this way because they would end up looking drab.

Pan-Frying

This is a last-minute technique enjoyed by creative, action-minded cooks. The hot frying pan seals the juices inside and produces a rapid transfer of heat into the fish's interior. You'll need a heavy 12-inch pan such as those manufactured by Viking, Silver Stone, All-Clad, and Calphalon.

To prevent splattering when adding the fish to the oiled pan, don't marinate the fish. Instead, add a protective layer such as a dusting of flour or cornstarch, or a more substantial layer of bread crumbs or ground nuts (see page 12).

Place the pan over medium-high heat. When hot, add 1 to 3 tablespoons peanut, safflower, or corn oil; olive oil; butter; or any combination of these. Butter will help the fish turn a more beautiful brown.

Roll the oil/butter around the sides of the pan so that the surface and sides are evenly coated.

When the oil gives off just a faint hint of smoke, add the fish. To prevent sticking, as soon as you add the fish, give the pan a slight jiggle so that the oil moves back under the fish.

Adjust the heat so the oil is always sizzling but is never smoking. Cook for 1 to 2 minutes, until the fish lightly browns on one side, then turn it over.

If the fish is to be cooked in a sauce, add the sauce and bring to a boil. Decrease the heat to low so the sauce simmers. For thick pieces of fish, cover the pan and simmer for 3 to 5 minutes, until done.

Pan-Frying/Roasting

The technique of combining pan-frying and roasting is often used by chefs. After pan-frying the fish until brown on one side (about 2 minutes), turn the fish over, and place the pan in a 300°F oven. Roast uncovered for 5 to 8 minutes, until done. The advantage of this technique is that the fish needs less supervision during cooking.

Stir-Frying

Stir-frying fish locks in flavors and glazes the surface of the fish with your sauce. You'll want to use a flat-bottom 14- or 16-inch-diameter heavy wok with one long wooden handle and one short handle.

Never stir-fry more than 1 pound of fish or 4 cups of vegetables at a time. If you want to stir-fry a larger amount, use two woks or sauté pans.

Heat the wok over the highest possible heat until very hot. Tap the sides of the wok with your fingers to make sure it is evenly heated. Add 1 tablespoon of peanut, safflower, or corn oil to the center of the wok, and roll the oil quickly around the bottom third.

When the oil just begins to give off a wisp of smoke, add any firm fish (see page 13) that has been cut into very thin, bite-sized pieces. Stir-fry the fish until the color changes, about 1 minute. If there are no vegetables, add the sauce and bring to a low boil so that it thickens. Slide the fish onto a serving plate or dinner plates.

If the stir-fry includes vegetables, remove the fish from the wok after its preliminary cooking. Immediately return the wok to high heat and add 1 more tablespoon peanut, safflower, or corn oil. When the oil is hot, add the vegetables. Stir-fry until the vegetables brighten in color. Return the fish to the wok, pour in the sauce, and stir-fry for about 1 more minute until the sauce glazes the vegetables and fish.

Take note, however, that flaky fish (see page 13) is not given a preliminary stir-frying because the fish quickly breaks apart into little pieces. Cut flaky fish into larger, bite-sized pieces. Heat the wok over high heat and add the oil. When the oil is hot, add the vegetables and fish. Stir-fry for 1 minute, then add the sauce and cover the wok. Lift the lid every 30 seconds, stir briefly, and then cover. When the vegetables turn a bright color, the fish loses its raw color, and the sauce fully glazes the ingredients, transfer the food to plates or a serving platter.

Poaching

Poaching is a gentle method for cooking fish that requires little supervision. The fish can be served hot or warm, but it has the most flavor when chilled and served cold.

In a large, shallow saucepan, simmer water, wine, or chicken broth (or a combination of these) with spices, herbs, and flavorings such as citrus slices for about 20 minutes. This infuses the liquid with flavor. Be sure there is enough liquid to completely cover the fish when it is added.

Gently add the fish to the simmering liquid. Turn off the heat and cover the pan. You can keep the pan on the burner or remove it from the stove. Fish that is $\frac{1}{2}$ inch thick should be done in 8 minutes; fish that is 1 inch thick should be ready in 15 minutes.

Carefully remove the fish with spatulas.

Steaming

The Asian steaming technique traps steam around the fish, cooking it slowly and delicately.

Shape a sheet of aluminum foil into a sling. Rub the top surface with oil to prevent the fish from sticking. Place the fish in the sling. If you don't want any moisture to accumulate around the fish, then keep the foil flat. Or cup the foil slightly to trap the moisture during steaming.

Pour enough water into a frying pan or wok so that it will not boil away (about 2 inches deep). Bring to a boil over high heat. Place the foil sling holding the fish on a steamer rack. Place the rack on the frying pan or wok and cover with the lid. When the fish is cooked (see page 12), grab the ends of the foil (the ends will be cool to the touch), lift the fish out, and slide the fish off the foil onto dinner plates.

Improvise a steamer using a tart pan ring or a collapsible vegetable steamer that is placed inside a large pan.

Microwaving

Microwaving is fast and simple, and it yields phenomenally moist fish. No guilt or apologies, please. Quantity is the only drawback when microwaving fish since you can't evenly cook more than two 8-ounce fillets or steaks. This is a technique to use only when cooking for two people.

Rub the fish with an oil and vinegar dressing, any marinade, or flavor it simply with a scattering of salt, freshly ground black pepper, olive oil, and a squeeze of fresh lemon juice.

Place the fish on a plate in a single layer with the thicker sides facing outward. Cover with a domed microwave lid or loosely wrap the plate with parchment paper or plastic wrap. Cook at full power for 2 minutes.

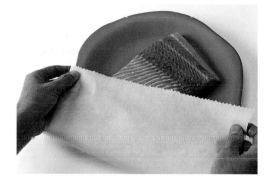

Remove the lid, turn the fish over, cover, and cook for 1 minute. Continue cooking at full power in 1-minute intervals, turning the fish over and covering it again, until the fish begins to flake easily when prodded with a fork. The total cooking time for a 1-inch-thick piece of fish should be around 3 minutes.

Essential Equipment

Barbecue Spatulas

Offset spatulas (the handle is higher than the spatula surface) are the best for barbecuing because they keep your hand away from the heat.

Electric Mini-Choppers

Use the mini-chopper for mincing ginger, garlic, fresh chiles, shallots, and green onions. To mince ginger, thoroughly wash or peel away the skin with a paring knife. Cut the ginger crosswise into paper-thin slices, and mince in the chopper. Don't use the electric mini-chopper for herbs because the blade will tear and it blackens the leaves. To mince herbs, just bunch the herbs together with your fingers and mince with a knife. The best mini-chopper brands are Krups and Cuisinart.

Fish Scalers

There are numerous fish scalers available. The one made by Westmark has a useful trap to collect the loosened scales. To minimize flying scales, you can scale the fish inside a large plastic bag.

Fish Screens

Fish screens to hold fillets, steaks, and whole fish are extremely useful for barbecuing because they prevent the fish from sticking to the grill. Be sure to buy a nonstick screen or the fish will stick to the screen. It's important also that the screen have a detachable handle so that the barbecue lid can be closed. It's easy to forget that the handle can get fiery hot.

Fish Spatulas

These thinly webbed spatulas work wonderfully for turning fish over in a sauté pan. Steel fish spatulas are more pliable and easier to use than plastic fish spatulas.

Fish Tweezers and Pliers

To remove pin bones, it's easier to use the straight-edged fish tweezers than the fish pliers.

Garlic Press

The Zyliss Garlic Press is by far the best. You don't have to peel the garlic: just place the cloves with their skin in the socket. Press down on the plunger to force the garlic through the holes. Then lift up the plunger and remove the skin. The garlic press also works for ginger. Cut the ginger crosswise (never lengthwise) in paper-thin slices. Stand the slices on edge in the socket and then press the plunger down.

Instant-Read Thermometer

Of the dozens of food thermometers, the battery-operated ones are the most accurate. We like the Polder and Component Design (CDN), with the long probe and the large dial. Except for tuna, which should be served raw to medium-rare, all other fish are properly cooked when they reach an internal temperature of 135°F to 140°F.

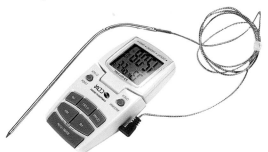

Juicers

Small amounts of juice are extracted quickest by using a reamer or a small plastic juicer.

Microplanes and Graters

These are handy gadgets for efficiently grating citrus skin or small amounts of cheese. Our favorite brand is the Great Zester made by Cuisipro.

Olive Pitters

Using an olive pitter is easier and more effective than pitting with a sharp knife. The best olive pitters are the Westmark and Pedrini models.

Skinning Knife

It's important that the knife be straight edged, flexible, and slightly longer than the width of the fish.

Essential Pantry

Good cooking begins with great ingredients. This means not only purchasing the freshest vegetables, seafood, meats, and herbs, but also choosing the best types of oils, vinegars, and seasonings. In terms of Asian condiments, the best brands are sold in Chinese, Vietnamese, and Thai markets. If you are unsure where the nearest Asian market is located, just ask the owner of your favorite Asian restaurant.

Bread Crumbs, Dry: Though you can make your own bread crumbs from stale bread, store-bought crumbs are more convenient and are readily found in supermarkets. Use unseasoned finely ground bread crumbs, or substitute Japanese bread crumbs, called panko. Panko, which can be found in most supermarkets, are coarser, resulting in a crunchy crust.

Butter: Always use unsalted butter, never margarine or other butter substitutes. Acceptable substitutes are: flavorless cooking oil (such as peanut, safflower, or corn oil) or olive oil.

Capers: The flower bud of a bush native to the Mediterranean and parts of Asia, capers are sold pickled in a vinegar brine. Rinse and drain before using.

Cheeses: There are many small manufacturers of excellent American goat cheese (such as Laura Chenel, from California) and Maytag blue cheese, but American-produced Parmesan has a scalded milk taste. Always use Italian Parmigiano-Reggiano cheese in recipes.

Chicken Broth: While we prefer using the frozen chicken broth available in some supermarkets, Swanson Low-Sodium Chicken Broth or boxed organic chicken broth can also be used.

Chiles: The smaller the fresh chile, the spicier its taste. To use, discard the stem, and then mince the chile, without removing the seeds, in an electric mini-chopper.

Chile Sauce, Asian: There are many types of Asian chile sauces made from just chiles, not including tomatoes. A favorite of ours is Rooster Brand Delicious Hot Chili Garlic Sauce. You should use your favorite brand wherever called for in the book.

Chipotle Chiles in Adobo Sauce: These smoked jalapeños simmered in a spicy sauce are sold in 4-ounce tins at Latin American markets and in many supermarkets. To use, finely mince the chiles, including the seeds, and use along with the sauce. A word of warning: these are extremely spicy. To store, transfer to a glass or sealable plastic container and refrigerate. The chiles will last indefinitely.

Crushed Red Peppers: Dried chile flakes are sold in the spice section of supermarkets.

Ginger: These pungent and spicy knobby brown roots are found in the produce section of supermarkets. Buy firm ginger with smooth skin. It isn't necessary to peel ginger unless the skin is wrinkled. Unpeeled ginger should be thoroughly washed. Store uncut fresh ginger in the refrigerator or at room temperature.

Hoisin Sauce: Hoisin sauce is a thick, sweet, spicy, dark condiment made with soybeans, chiles, garlic, ginger, and sugar. Once opened, it keeps indefinitely at room temperature. Our preferred brand is Koon Chun.

Coconut Milk: This ingredient is used to add flavor and body to sauces. Always purchase a milk that is composed entirely of coconut and water. Stir or shake the coconut milk before using. Our favorite brand is Chaokoh, from Thailand. Once opened, coconut milk should be kept for only 5 days in the refrigerator. It can also be frozen. Never substitute lowfat coconut milk; it tastes terrible.

Fish Sauce: Made from fermenting anchovies or other fish in a brine, fish sauce is used in Thai and Vietnamese cooking the way the Chinese use soy sauce. Always buy fish sauce produced in Thailand or Vietnam since these sauces have the lowest salt content. Once opened, fish sauce lasts indefinitely at room temperature. Our favorite brands are Three Crab, Phu Quoc Flying Lion, and Tiparos. Thin, or light, soy sauce can be substituted, although the flavor is quite different.

Herbs: Available throughout the year at most supermarkets, fresh herbs have a far more intense bouquet than their dried counterparts. In an emergency, dried herbs can be substituted for fresh herbs; use about half the amount of fresh. To prepare most fresh herbs, separate the leaves from the stems, discard the stems, and then chop or mince the leaves. The exception to this procedure is cilantro—both stems and leaves are used.

Oil: For sautéing and general cooking it's best to use a flavorless cooking oil with a high smoking temperature, such as canola, peanut, safflower, and corn. However, some Mediterranean dishes benefit in flavor by using extra virgin olive oil.

Oyster Sauce: This Asian cooking sauce gives dishes a rich taste without providing even a hint of its seafood origins. It will keep indefinitely in the refrigerator. Our favorite brands are Sa Cheng Oyster Flavored Sauce; Hop Sing Lung Oyster Sauce; and Lee Kum Kee Oyster Flavored Sauce, Old Brand.

Pomegranate Molasses (or Pomegranate Syrup): This is a deep cherry–colored liquid with the consistency of syrup and a sweet, tart, and fruity taste. It's delicious on pancakes, in salad dressing, and rubbed on fish about to come off the barbecue. It's available in most Middle Eastern markets and gourmet food shops.

Sesame Oil, Dark: This nutty, dark golden brown oil is made from toasted and crushed white sesame seeds. Dark sesame oil shouldn't be mistaken for clear-colored sesame oil made from untoasted sesame seeds, which is flavorless, or for black sesame oil, which has far too strong a taste. Dark sesame oil will last for at least a year at room temperature and indefinitely in the refrigerator. Our favorite is Kadoya Sesame Oil.

Olives: Buy only imported olives—black or green, seed-in or pitted. It's more convenient to use pitted olives, but the unpitted ones have more flavor.

Olive Tapenade: This is a thick paste that can sometimes be found in higher-end supermarkets. To make ⅓ cup of tapenade, combine ½ cup pitted black olives, 2 cloves garlic, 1 tablespoon lemon juice, and 1 tablespoon olive oil in a food processor.

Peppercorns, Tricolor: You can find this mix of black, white, pink, and green peppercorns on the spice rack of most supermarkets. The mixture offers a more complex flavor than straight black pepper. To use, grind in a spice or pepper grinder.

Red Peppers, Roasted: Red bell peppers take on a sweet, smoky flavor when roasted, peeled, and seeded. They are available bottled and are sold alongside the pickles and relishes at most supermarkets.

Sesame Seeds, White: White sesame seeds are sold in the spice section of supermarkets. Avoid pretoasted or brown seeds, which are inferior in taste.

Sherry, Dry: Always use good-quality dry sherry or Chinese rice wine (not to be confused with rice wine vinegar). We like Pagoda Brand Shao Xing Rice Wine. White wine or sake can be substituted, if necessary.

Tomatoes: Many of our recipes call for vine-ripened tomatoes. If you cannot find good-quality fresh tomatoes, substitute shelf-stable chopped or puréed tomatoes. Choose bottled or boxed brands such as Pomi, Classico, Muir Glen, and Newman's Own. Do not buy canned tomato products, which have a metallic taste.

Vinegar, Japanese Rice: This vinegar, made from fermented rice, is slightly milder than Western vinegar, with 4 to 5 percent acidity compared to the 6 to 7 percent in Western vinegars. If a recipe calls for rice vinegar but all you have is a red or white wine vinegar, use a little less than called for in the recipe. Rice vinegar is available in Asian markets and most supermarkets.

Wood Chips: Wood chips add a complex flavor to barbecued fish. There is no correct type of wood to match with a particular fish. Experiment with hickory, apple wood, pecan, and other types of chips. Do not substitute any soft types of wood such as pine or fir. For instructions on how to use wood chips, see page 13.

Soy Sauce, Thin: The mildly salty "thin," or "light," soy sauce is made from soybeans, roasted wheat, yeast, and salt. Our favorites are Pearl River Bridge Golden Label Superior Soya Sauce, Koon Chun Thin Soy Sauce, and Kikkoman Regular Soy Sauce.

Vinegar, Balsamic: The best balsamic vinegars are made in Modena, Italy, from Trebbiano grapes. These vinegars are aged for a minimum of twelve years, and are more expensive than other balsamic vinegars. Recipes in this book use the more pedestrian balsamic vinegar, which you can find in supermarkets for about $10 for an 8-ounce bottle.

Wasabi: This is the dried, powdered, and artificially colored root of a Japanese plant similar to horseradish. When mixed into a thin paste using water or beer, it is very spicy. Wasabi powder and paste are sold in the Asian foods section of most supermarkets.

Black Cod (Sablefish)

Covered with a black, furry skin, black cod is known to the Chinese as "gopher fish." Of course it is not a gopher, but it's not a cod either. The black cod is a member of the skilfish family. Its high fat content makes it an excellent fish for smoking and perfect for a wide variety of cooking techniques. Even when overcooked, its richly flavored flesh will be moist. Black cod is sometimes sold as "butterfish" because of its rich texture. (However, it has no relation to authentic butterfish, a small fish labeled as Pacific pompano, harvest fish, or star butterfish in Asian markets.) Black cod is fished in deep waters from the Pacific Northwest to Alaska from January to October; it is also farmed. Although it can weigh as much as 40 pounds, in markets black cod ranges in weight from 3 to 10 pounds.

SUBSTITUTES:
black sea bass, grouper, pollack, rockfish, salmon (all varieties), snapper, tilapia, walleyed pike

RECOMMENDED COOKING TECHNIQUES:
barbecue, braise, broil, deep-fry, microwave, pan-fry, poach, roast, steam

Pan-Fried Black Cod with Tomatoes and Olives

SERVES 4

1 cup chicken broth
⅓ cup imported pitted black olives, chopped
2 vine-ripened tomatoes, chopped
⅓ cup basil leaves, torn into small pieces
2 tablespoons grated lemon zest
2 teaspoons cornstarch
½ teaspoon salt
¼ teaspoon freshly ground black pepper
1½ pounds black cod fillets, skinned
¼ cup all-purpose flour
¼ cup extra virgin olive oil
2 tablespoons unsalted butter
3 cloves garlic, chopped

In a bowl, combine the broth, olives, tomatoes, basil, lemon zest, cornstarch, salt, and pepper and mix well. (The broth mixture can be covered and refrigerated for up to 8 hours before using.)

Working in batches or using 2 large sauté pans, place the pans over medium-high heat. Sprinkle salt and pepper on both sides of the fish. Lightly dust both sides of the fish with the flour, shaking off the excess. Place the oil and butter in the pan. When the butter begins to brown, add the fish, curved side down. Cook, turning once, for about 2 minutes on each side, until the fish just begins to flake when prodded with a spatula. Transfer the fish to dinner plates.

Return 1 of the sauté pans to medium-high heat. Add the garlic and sauté for 15 seconds. Add the broth mixture and bring to a boil. Immediately spoon the sauce over the fish and serve at once.

Barbecued Coconut-Pineapple Black Cod

SERVES 4

1½ cups unsweetened coconut milk
1 tablespoon Asian chile sauce
1½ teaspoons curry powder
¾ teaspoon salt
3 tablespoons minced fresh ginger
2 cloves garlic, minced
3 tablespoons chopped fresh mint
3 tablespoons chopped cilantro sprigs
2 teaspoons grated lime zest
1½ pounds black cod fillets, skinned
¼ fresh pineapple, peeled, cored, and cut crosswise
    into paper-thin slices

In a bowl, combine the coconut milk, chile sauce, curry powder, salt, ginger, garlic, mint, cilantro, and lime zest and mix well. (The marinade can be covered and refrigerated for up to 8 hours before using.)

Place a sheet of aluminum foil on the grill rack. Prepare a medium-hot fire in a charcoal grill or preheat a gas grill to medium (about 450°F). Place the fish in a baking dish. Stir the marinade and pour half of it over the fish. Turn the fish to coat evenly. Place the fish in the refrigerator to marinate for 5 to 15 minutes.

Arrange the pineapple in a single layer on the foil in the barbecue. Remove the fish from the marinade, and discard the marinade. Place the fish flat side down on the pineapple. Cover the grill and cook for 6 minutes before lifting the lid. If the fish does not flake when prodded with a fork, close the lid and cook for 2 minutes more. When the fish is done, transfer the pineapple and fish to dinner plates.

In a small saucepan, bring the remaining marinade to a low boil over medium-high heat. Spoon the sauce over the fish and serve at once.

Pan-Roasted Black Cod with Herb Rub

SERVES 4

2 tablespoons chopped fresh basil
2 tablespoons chopped cilantro sprigs
2 tablespoons minced green onion
2 tablespoons toasted white sesame seeds (see page 68)
3 cloves garlic, minced
2 tablespoons minced fresh ginger
½ teaspoon crushed red pepper flakes
½ teaspoon salt
1½ pounds black cod fillets, skinned
¼ cup extra virgin olive oil
¼ cup unsalted butter
4 lemon wedges

In a bowl, combine the basil, cilantro, green onion, sesame seeds, garlic, ginger, pepper flakes, and salt and mix well.

Preheat the oven to 300°F. Rub the curved side of the fillets with olive oil. Rub the herb mix on top. Place 2 large ovenproof sauté pans over medium-high heat. When hot, add 1 tablespoon of the butter to each pan. When the butter melts, add the fish, curved side down. Pan-fry for 1 minute, and then turn the fish over. Transfer the sauté pans to the oven. Cook for about 8 minutes, until the flesh just begins to flake when prodded with a fork. Transfer the fish to dinner plates.

Return 1 of the sauté pans to the stove over medium heat and melt the remaining 2 tablespoons butter. Drizzle the melted butter over the fish. Serve at once, accompanied by the lemon wedges.

Cod is a popular saltwater fish found on both the Atlantic and Pacific Coasts. Fish in the cod family include haddock, Atlantic pollack (or blue cod or Boston bluefish), hake/whiting, Alaskan pollack, and Pacific cod (or true cod or gray cod). Black cod (sablefish), rock cod (rockfish), and lingcod (greenling) are totally unrelated to the cod family. Cod has white, flaky, mild-flavored, delicate-tasting flesh. It's a versatile fish that can be cooked using virtually any cooking method.

Pine Nut-Crusted Black Cod

SERVES 4

4 ounces Parmigiano-Reggiano cheese
1 cup toasted pine nuts (see sidebar)
2 tablespoons dried Italian seasoning
1 teaspoon salt
½ cup all-purpose flour
1½ pounds black cod fillets, skinned
3 eggs, beaten
½ cup balsamic vinegar
½ cup freshly squeezed orange juice
2 tablespoons honey
2 cloves garlic, minced
¼ to ½ teaspoon crushed red pepper flakes
⅓ cup chopped fresh parsley, for garnish

Place the cheese in the bowl of a food processor and process until finely ground. Add the pine nuts, Italian seasoning, and ½ teaspoon of the salt and finely chop. Spread the nut mixture and the flour on separate plates. Dip both sides of the fish in the flour and shake off the excess. Dip the fish into the eggs, and then coat evenly with the nut mixture. (The battered fish can be covered and refrigerated for up to 8 hours before using.)

Preheat the oven to 400°F. Place the fish in a baking dish, flat side down. Roast for 12 to 14 minutes, until it just begins to flake.

In a saucepan over medium-high heat, combine the vinegar, orange juice, honey, garlic, pepper flakes, and the remaining ½ teaspoon salt. Bring to a boil for about 1 minute, until slightly thickened. Transfer the fish to dinner plates and drizzle with the sauce. Sprinkle with the parsley and serve at once.

(Photographed at right)

TOASTING PINE NUTS

Preheat the oven to 325°F. Spread the pine nuts in an ovenproof sauté pan and place in the oven. Toast for about 8 minutes, until golden. Remove from the oven and set aside to cool.

Pan-Fried Black Cod with Salsa

SERVES 4

4 cups white corn tortilla chips
½ cup all-purpose flour
1½ pounds black cod fillets, skinned
Salt and freshly ground black pepper
3 eggs, beaten
3 tablespoons olive oil
2 tablespoons unsalted butter
1 recipe Mexican Salsa, at room temperature (page 107)

Place the tortilla chips in the bowl of a food processor and process until finely ground (you will have about 1 cup). Spread the ground chips and flour on separate plates. Sprinkle both sides of the fish with salt and pepper. Coat the fish on both sides with flour and shake off the excess. Dip the fish in the eggs, and then coat on both sides with the ground chips. (The battered fish can be covered and refrigerated for up to 8 hours before using.)

Working in batches or using 2 large sauté pans, place the pans over medium heat. When hot, add the oil and butter. When the butter begins to brown, add the fish, curved side down. Cook for about 2 minutes, until the underside browns. Turn the fish over, cover the pan, and decrease the heat to low. Cook for 2 minutes, until the fish just begins to flake when prodded with a fork. If the fish is not done, cover the pan and cook for 2 minutes more. Transfer to dinner plates. Spoon the salsa over the fish and serve at once.

Pan-Roasted Black Cod with Andouille Sausage

SERVES 4

1 cup chopped andouille sausage or cured spicy sausage
2 tablespoons chopped shallot
4 cloves garlic, minced
2 tomatoes, chopped, or ½ cup bottled or boxed
    chopped tomatoes
2 small hot chiles, minced, including seeds
1 tablespoon chopped fresh oregano, or 1 teaspoon
    chopped fresh thyme
½ teaspoon salt
1 cup dry white wine
3 tablespoons extra virgin olive oil
1½ pounds black cod fillets, skinned
¼ cup chopped fresh parsley, for garnish

Place the sausage, shallot, and garlic in a bowl and mix to combine evenly. In a separate bowl, combine the tomatoes, chiles, oregano, salt, and wine and mix well. (The sausage and tomato mixtures can be covered and refrigerated for up to 8 hours before using.)

Working in batches or using 2 large sauté pans, place the pans over medium-high heat and add the olive oil. When the oil is hot, add the sausage mixture. Cook for about 2 minutes, until the shallots are translucent. Add the tomato mixture and stir to evenly combine. Add the fish flat side down in a single layer. Cover the pan and decrease the heat to low. Cook for 8 minutes, until the fish just begins to flake. If the fish is not done, cover the pan and cook for 1 minute more. Transfer the fish to dinner plates and spoon the sauce over. Sprinkle with the parsley and serve at once.

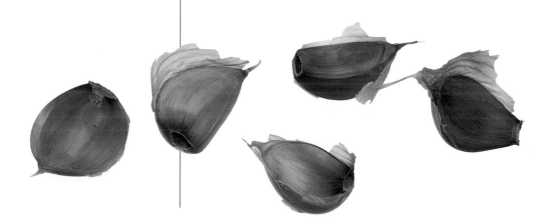

Poached Black Cod with Lemon-Dill Mayonnaise

SERVES 4

2 cups dry white wine
2 cups water
1/2 cup plus 2 teaspoons freshly squeezed lemon juice
5 lemon slices
1/2 cup dill sprigs
2 teaspoons salt
1 teaspoon tricolor peppercorns
1 1/2 pounds black cod fillets, skinned
1/4 cup mayonnaise
2 teaspoons chopped fresh dill
1 teaspoon grated lemon zest
1/2 teaspoon freshly ground black pepper
2 cups shredded unpeeled cucumber

In a saucepan or sauté pan just large enough to hold the fish, combine the wine, water, 1/2 cup of the lemon juice, the lemon slices, dill sprigs, salt, and peppercorns. Place over high heat and bring to a boil. Decrease the heat to low, cover, and simmer for 20 minutes. Add the fish, ensuring that it is completely submerged. Cover the pan and turn off the heat (you can leave the pan on the burner or remove from the stove). After 20 minutes, remove the fish from the liquid and discard the liquid. Place the fish on a plate, cover, and refrigerate for at least 1 hour and up to 8 hours before serving. In a bowl, combine the mayonnaise, chopped dill, lemon zest, the remaining lemon juice, and the black pepper and stir well. (The mayonnaise can be covered and refrigerated for up to 8 hours before using.)

Divide the cucumber evenly among 4 dinner plates. Place the fish on top of the cucumber, dividing evenly. Top the fish with spoonfuls of the mayonnaise. Serve at room temperature or chilled.

Broiled Black Cod with Vanilla, Butter, and Walnuts

SERVES 4

1/4 cup chopped walnuts
1 1/2 pounds black cod fillets, skinned
1/2 teaspoon salt
1 teaspoon tricolor peppercorns, finely ground, or freshly ground black pepper
1 teaspoon vanilla bean paste or pure vanilla extract
3 tablespoons unsalted butter, cut into small pieces
1/4 cup chopped fresh parsley or mint, for garnish
1 tablespoon freshly squeezed lemon juice

Preheat the oven to 325°F. Spread the walnuts on a small ungreased baking sheet and toast, stirring occasionally, for about 15 minutes, until darkened.

Line a baking sheet with aluminum foil. Rub the fish on both sides with the salt and peppercorns. Rub the curved side with the vanilla. Place the fish flat side down on the foil. Dot the fish with the pieces of butter. Position an oven rack 4 inches from the heating element and turn the oven to broil. Immediately place the fish in the oven and cook for about 4 minutes, until it begins to brown. The flesh should flake easily when prodded with a fork. If the fish is not done, turn the oven to bake at 300°F and cook for about 2 minutes. Check again for doneness. Transfer the fish to dinner plates, spooning any butter that has collected in the pan over the fish. Sprinkle with the walnuts, parsley, and lemon juice. Serve at once.

VANILLA BEAN PASTE

Vanilla bean paste is made from pure vanilla extract and ground vanilla beans. With its syruplike consistency, it can be used interchangeably and in the same amount as vanilla extract. It is sold in gourmet shops and high-end supermarkets.

Roasted Black Cod with Indian Spices

SERVES 4

1 teaspoon ground coriander
1 teaspoon ground nutmeg
1 teaspoon ground cayenne pepper
1/2 teaspoon ground cinnamon
1 teaspoon salt
1 teaspoon ground cumin
1 1/2 pounds black cod fillets, skinned
3 cloves garlic, minced
1/4 cup olive oil
1/2 cup packed mint leaves
1/2 cup packed cilantro sprigs
1/3 cup plain yogurt
2 tablespoons freshly squeezed lemon juice
2 tablespoons honey

In a bowl, combine the coriander, nutmeg, cayenne, cinnamon, 1/2 teaspoon of the salt, and 1/2 teaspoon of the cumin. Rub both sides of the fish with the garlic and then with the spice mixture, and then with the olive oil. In the bowl of a food processor, combine the remaining 1/2 teaspoon salt, the remaining 1/2 teaspoon cumin, the mint, cilantro, yogurt, lemon juice, and honey. Process until evenly blended. (The fish and the yogurt sauce can be covered and refrigerated for up to 8 hours before using. Bring the sauce to room temperature before serving.)

Preheat the oven to 400°F. Place the fish flat side down in a baking dish. Place uncovered in the oven and roast for 12 to 14 minutes, until the fish just begins to flake when prodded with a fork. Transfer to dinner plates, spoon on the sauce, and serve at once.

(Photographed at left)

Plank-Smoked Black Cod with Dill and Ginger

SERVES 4

1 (4 by 12-inch) cedar or alder plank
1/2 cup chopped fresh dill
2 tablespoons grated lemon zest
1/2 cup freshly squeezed lemon juice
1/2 cup packed brown sugar
1/2 cup extra virgin olive oil
1/2 teaspoon salt
1 tablespoon freshly ground black pepper
2 tablespoons minced fresh ginger
1 1/2 pounds black cod fillets, skinned

Submerge the plank in cold water for 8 to 24 hours. Set aside 1 tablespoon of the dill. In a bowl, combine the remaining dill, the lemon zest, lemon juice, sugar, oil, salt, pepper, and ginger. (The marinade can be covered and refrigerated for up to 8 hours before using.)

Prepare a medium-hot fire in a charcoal grill or preheat a gas grill to medium (about 450°F). Place the fish in a baking dish and add the marinade. Turn the fish to coat evenly. Cover and place in the refrigerator for 5 to 15 minutes. Place the prepared plank on the grill rack. When the plank begins to smoke, place the fish flat side down on the plank. Cover the grill and cook for 10 minutes before lifting the lid. If the fish does not flake when prodded with a fork, close the lid and cook for 2 minutes more and check for doneness. Transfer to dinner plates and sprinkle with the reserved dill. Serve at once

PLANK COOKING

Place the wood plank in a roasting pan, cover with cold water, and submerge by placing a large pot of water on top of the plank. Soak the plank for 8 to 24 hours to prevent it from being flammable on the barbecue. The plank can be used several times as long as the soaking process is repeated just prior to the next use.

Purchase cedar or alder planks at cookware shops, not at lumberyards, where the wood may be saturated with fire-retardant chemicals.

Barbecued Black Cod Tostados

SERVES 4

Honey-Lime Salad Dressing
¹/₂ cup freshly squeezed lime juice
¹/₂ cup extra virgin olive oil
¹/₄ cup honey
2 fresh hot chiles, minced, including seeds
1 teaspoon ground cumin
¹/₂ teaspoon salt
2 small garlic cloves, minced
¹/₄ cup chopped cilantro sprigs or fresh basil

1¹/₂ pounds black cod fillets, skinned
4 store-bought crisp tostado shells
1 small head iceberg lettuce, shredded (4 cups)
1 avocado, sliced
1 red onion, thinly sliced
2 vine-ripened tomatoes, chopped
1 cup Mexican Salsa (page 107)
1 cup grated Jack cheese

Prepare a medium-hot fire in a charcoal grill or preheat a gas grill to medium (about 450°F). In a bowl, combine all of the ingredients for the salad dressing and mix well.

Place the fish in a baking dish and add half of the dressing. Turn the fish to coat evenly. Brush the grill rack with oil. Place the fish on the rack and grill, turning once, for 3 minutes on each side, until it just begins to flake. Transfer the fish to a cutting board and slice into 8 strips.

Place a tostado shell on each plate. In a bowl, combine the lettuce, avocado, and onion and toss well. Arrange the lettuce mixture on the tostado shells. Drizzle with the remaining salad dressing. Top with the strips of fish. Sprinkle with the tomatoes, salsa, and cheese and serve at once.

(Photographed at right)

Rockfish is the largest of Pacific Coast fish families, with more than fifty varieties. This lowfat fish is sometimes marketed as Pacific snapper, Pacific red snapper, and rock cod, but they are not related to the true Atlantic snapper. To make matters more confusing, striped bass is sometimes referred to as rockfish. Rockfish are a deepwater fish with brightly colored skin and firm flesh. They average from 5 to 15 pounds. Unfortunately, most commercially caught "Pacific snapper" is low in fat with a coarse texture. We've had varieties caught by sportfishermen that taste wonderful. Rockfish is best barbecued, broiled, roasted, braised, and steamed.

Catfish

Catfish is one of the best tasting and most versatile fish sold in markets today. It is firm-fleshed, low in fat, and mild in flavor. When displayed whole, it's a scary-looking fish, with its long whiskers ("barbels," or feelers) dangling from around the mouth. There's still some prejudice against eating catfish based on childhood memories of a murky, muddy taste. That's because catfish was often pulled out of rivers in the American South. Now nearly all catfish is farm raised and hasn't even a hint of muddiness. Although there are more than 2,000 species of catfish, it's the farm-raised channel catfish species that you'll find in the market. Whether cut into steaks or filleted, catfish is always sold with the tough, inedible skin removed.

SUBSTITUTES:
black cod (sablefish), black sea bass, lemon sole, rockfish, salmon (all varieties),
snapper, tilapia, walleyed pike

RECOMMENDED COOKING TECHNIQUES:
barbecue, braise, broil, pan-fry, roast, steam

Barbecued Catfish with Pomegranate Sauce

SERVES 4

¼ cup chopped walnuts
8 oranges, unpeeled
⅔ cup pomegranate molasses
¼ cup extra virgin olive oil
½ teaspoon salt
½ teaspoon freshly ground black pepper
3 cloves garlic, minced
⅓ cup chopped fresh chives or parsley
4 (6-ounce) catfish fillets
⅓ cup fresh pomegranate seeds (optional)

Preheat the oven to 325°F. Spread the walnuts on a small ungreased baking sheet and toast, stirring occasionally, for about 15 minutes, until darkened. Cut 5 of the oranges into ¼-inch-thick slices. From the remaining 3 oranges, grate 2 teaspoons of orange zest and squeeze ⅔ cup of orange juice. In a bowl, combine the orange zest, orange juice, pomegranate molasses, olive oil, salt, pepper, garlic, and half of the chives. Stir well. (The sliced oranges and marinade can be covered and refrigerated for up to 8 hours before using. Store the walnuts at room temperature.)

Prepare a medium-hot fire in a charcoal grill or preheat a gas grill to medium (about 450°F). Rub the pomegranate mixture on both sides of the fish. Place the fish in a baking dish, cover, and refrigerate for 15 minutes. Lay the orange slices in a tight single layer directly on the grill rack. Place the fish on top of the orange slices. Cover the grill and cook for 8 minutes before lifting the lid. If the fish does not flake when prodded with a fork, close the lid and cook for 2 minutes more. Slide a spatula between the fish and orange slices and transfer the fish to dinner plates. Sprinkle with the walnuts, remaining chives, and pomegranate seeds and serve at once.

POMEGRANATE SEEDS

To remove the seeds from a pomegranate, cut the pomegranate in half. Submerge the halves in a bowl of cold water and use your fingers to dislodge the seeds. Pour the water and seeds through a sieve and discard any membrane and outer shell. The seeds can be refrigerated for up to 1 week.

Stir-Fried Spicy Catfish

SERVES 2 TO 3

⅓ cup chicken broth
2 tablespoons oyster sauce
1 tablespoon Asian chile sauce
1 tablespoon dark sesame oil
1 tablespoon grated lemon zest
2 teaspoons cornstarch
½ teaspoon sugar
¼ cup chopped cilantro sprigs or fresh mint
2 tablespoons peanut, safflower, or corn oil
3 cloves garlic, minced
1 pound catfish fillets, cut into 1-inch cubes

In a bowl, combine the broth, oyster sauce, chile sauce, sesame oil, lemon zest, cornstarch, sugar, and cilantro and mix well. (The sauce can be covered and refrigerated for up to 8 hours before using.)

Place a wok over high heat. When hot, add the oil. When the oil just begins to smoke, add the garlic and fish. Stir-fry for 2 minutes, until the fish loses its raw outside color. Stir the sauce and pour it into the wok. Continue stir-frying for 1 minute, until the fish just begins to flake. Transfer to dinner plates and serve at once.

Mexican Broiled Catfish

SERVES 4

½ cup chopped vine-ripened tomatoes
⅓ cup chopped cilantro sprigs
2 to 3 tablespoons roasted garlic (see sidebar), mashed
2 teaspoons minced chipotle chiles in adobo sauce
1 teaspoon cumin seeds
½ teaspoon salt
1 ripe avocado
4 (6-ounce) catfish fillets

In a bowl, combine the tomatoes, cilantro, garlic, chiles, cumin, and salt and stir well. (The marinade can be covered and refrigerated for up to 8 hours before using.)

Slice the avocado into 4 to 6 slices. Line a baking dish with aluminum foil. Place the fish flat side down on the foil. Spread the tomato mixture on top of each fillet. Position an oven rack 4 inches from the heating element and turn the oven to broil.

Immediately place the fish in the oven and cook for about 4 minutes, until it begins to brown. The flesh should flake easily when prodded with a fork. If the fish is not done, turn the oven to bake at 300°F and cook for about 2 minutes. Check again for doneness. Transfer to dinner plates and serve with the avocado slices.

(Photographed at left)

ROASTING GARLIC

To roast garlic, preheat the oven to 375°F. Cut off the top of the bulb using a serrated knife. Place the garlic in the center of a sheet of aluminum foil, drizzle the exposed garlic with extra virgin olive oil, seal the foil into a tent, and roast in the oven for 1 hour. When cool enough to handle, squeeze the garlic from the skin. A whole bulb should

yield about ¼ cup of garlic paste. Roasted garlic can be stored whole in the refrigerator for up to 2 weeks.

Asian Broiled Catfish

SERVES 4

¼ cup freshly squeezed lemon juice
¼ cup oyster sauce
¼ cup dry sherry or Chinese rice wine
1 tablespoon dark sesame oil
1 teaspoon Asian chile sauce
2 tablespoons minced fresh ginger
¼ cup minced green onion
4 (6-ounce) catfish fillets

In a bowl, combine the lemon juice, oyster sauce, sherry, sesame oil, chile sauce, ginger, and green onion and stir well. (The marinade can be covered and refrigerated for up to 8 hours before using.)

Place the fish in a baking dish and add the marinade. Turn the fish to coat evenly. Cover and refrigerate for 5 to 15 minutes. Line a baking dish with aluminum foil. Place the fish flat side down on the foil. Position an oven rack 4 inches from the heating element and turn the oven to broil. Immediately place the fish in the oven and cook for about 4 minutes, until it begins to brown. The flesh should flake easily when prodded with a fork. If the fish is not done, turn the oven to bake at 300°F and cook for about 2 minutes. Check again for doneness. Serve immediately.

Barbecued Catfish with Thyme

SERVES 4

4 (6-ounce) catfish fillets
2 to 4 cloves garlic, minced
2 tablespoons grated lemon zest (from 2 to 3 lemons)
½ teaspoon salt
½ teaspoon crushed red pepper flakes
1 tablespoon chopped fresh thyme, tarragon, or basil
¼ cup plus 1 tablespoon extra virgin olive oil

Rub the fish on both sides with the garlic, lemon zest, salt, pepper flakes, thyme, and the ¼ cup olive oil. Place in a baking dish, cover, and refrigerate for 5 to 15 minutes.

Prepare a medium-hot fire in a charcoal grill or preheat a gas grill to medium (about 450°F). Prepare a double layer of aluminum foil that is slightly larger than a single layer of the fish. Rub the foil with the remaining 1 tablespoon oil. Place the foil on the grill rack, oiled side up. Place the fish flat side down in a single layer on top of the foil. Cover the grill and cook for 8 minutes before lifting the lid. If the fish does not flake when prodded with a fork, close the lid and cook for 2 minutes more. Transfer the fish to dinner plates and serve at once.

New Orleans Pasta with Catfish

SERVES 3 TO 4

½ cup heavy whipping cream
½ cup dry sherry
6 tablespoons freshly squeezed lemon juice
2 tablespoons chopped fresh oregano
1 tablespoon Cajun hot sauce or your favorite hot sauce
½ teaspoon salt
8 ounces dried penne, fettuccine, or other dried pasta
¼ cup extra virgin olive oil
5 cloves garlic, chopped
3 (6-ounce) catfish fillets, cut into 1-inch cubes
½ cup pitted and chopped imported black olives
4 ounces Andouille sausage or any cured spicy sausage, chopped (about ½ cup)
2 ounces Parmigiano-Reggiano cheese, grated (about ¾ cup)
½ cup chopped fresh parsley, for garnish

In a bowl, combine the cream, sherry, lemon juice, oregano, hot sauce, and salt and mix well. (The sauce can be covered and refrigerated for up to 8 hours before using.)

Bring a large pot of water to a rapid boil over high heat. Lightly salt the water, add the pasta, and cook according to the package instructions until al dente. Drain well. Return the empty saucepan to the stove over high heat. Add the olive oil and garlic. When the garlic sizzles, add the sauce, pasta, fish, olives, and sausage. Stir for about 3 minutes, until the fish just begins to flake when prodded with a fork. Add the cheese and stir well. Transfer to dinner plates, sprinkle with the parsley, and serve at once.

(Photographed at right)

ANDOUILLE SAUSAGE

Andouille sausage is a heavily spiced smoked sausage much used in New Orleans cooking. A cured spicy Italian sausage or spicy salami is a good substitute.

Steamed Catfish with Ginger

SERVES 4

¼ cup Chinese rice wine or dry sherry
¼ cup thin soy sauce
2 tablespoons dark sesame oil
½ cup finely chopped green onions
¼ cup shredded fresh ginger
4 (6-ounce) catfish fillets
¼ cup peanut, safflower, or corn oil

In a bowl, combine the rice wine, soy sauce, sesame oil, green onions, and ginger and mix well. (The marinade can be covered and refrigerated for up to 8 hours before using.)

Place the fish in a baking dish. Stir the marinade and pour it over the fish. Turn the fish several times to evenly coat. Assemble a Chinese steamer (see page 17). Bring a large saucepan or sauté pan of water to a boil over high heat. Place a sheet of aluminum foil inside the steamer. Lay the fish flat side down on the foil in a single layer. Place the steamer tier over the boiling water and cover the steamer with its lid. Steam for 6 minutes, until the fish just begins to flake when prodded with a fork. Transfer the fish to dinner plates.

Heat a small saucepan over medium heat. As soon as the fish is transferred to the plates, add the peanut oil to the saucepan. Heat the oil for about 30 seconds, until it just begins to smoke. Immediately drizzle the hot oil over the fish and serve at once.

SHREDDING GINGER

To shred ginger, peel the ginger with a sharp knife and then cut it crosswise in very thin slices, about 1/16 inch thick. Overlap or stack the slices, and then cut into shreds.

Pan-Fried Catfish with Capers and Cream

SERVES 4

½ cup all-purpose flour
1 cup unseasoned dry bread crumbs or panko bread crumbs
4 (6-ounce) catfish fillets
3 eggs, beaten
⅓ cup bottled capers, rinsed and drained
½ cup chicken broth
½ cup heavy whipping cream
Juice of 1 lemon
½ teaspoon salt
¼ teaspoon freshly ground black pepper
¼ cup olive oil
2 tablespoons unsalted butter
3 small cloves garlic, thinly sliced
¼ cup chopped fresh parsley, for garnish

Spread the flour and bread crumbs on separate plates. Lightly dust the fish on both sides with the flour, dip in the eggs, and then evenly coat with the bread crumbs. Place the fish on a wire rack. In a bowl, combine the capers, broth, cream, lemon juice, salt and pepper and mix well. (The battered fish and the sauce can be covered and refrigerated for up to 8 hours before using.)

Using 2 large sauté pans or working in batches, heat the pans over medium-high heat. When the pan is hot, add the oil and butter. When the butter begins to brown, add the fish flat side up in a single layer. Cook, turning once, for 2 minutes on each side. The fish is done when it just begins to flake when prodded with the edge of a spatula. Transfer the fish to warmed dinner plates.

Return 1 of the pans to the stove over medium-high heat. Add the garlic to the pan and sauté for 15 seconds. Add the cream sauce and bring to a rapid boil. Spoon the sauce over the fish. Sprinkle with the parsley and serve at once.

(Photographed at right)

Halibut

Halibut, a member of the flatfish family, can be as large as half a ton. Like all flatfish, it lives on the ocean floor, and its bottom eye gradually migrates to the top side. The skin on the top side is a mottled black to brown color, designed to match the surrounding sand to protect the fish from predators. The California halibut is the smallest variety, weighing in at 4 to 12 pounds. Alaskan and Atlantic halibut have a firmer texture. Startlingly white, mild-tasting, and low in fat, this fish, which you'll find sold as fillets or steaks, is one of the most versatile fish to cook and adapts well to virtually all cooking techniques. Specialty markets occasionally sell halibut cheeks. With their higher fat content, the cheeks are divine grilled or pan-fried.

SUBSTITUTES:
black cod (sablefish), black sea bass, catfish, grouper, monkfish, rockfish, salmon (all varieties), snapper, striped bass, walleyed pike

RECOMMENDED COOKING TECHNIQUES:
barbecue, broil, pan-fry, poach, roast

Steamed Halibut with Garlic Blanket

SERVES 4

4 large heads roasted garlic (page 37)
¼ cup extra virgin olive oil
½ cup chopped cilantro sprigs
½ teaspoon salt
2 teaspoons crushed red pepper flakes
4 (6-ounce) halibut fillets
4 lemon wedges

Squeeze the garlic out of each clove. You should have about ⅔ cup of roasted garlic. In a bowl, combine the garlic, olive oil, cilantro, salt, and pepper flakes and mash to mix evenly. (The garlic paste can be covered and refrigerated for up to 8 hours before using.)

Assemble a Chinese steamer (see page 17). Bring a large saucepan or sauté pan of water to a boil over high heat. Place a layer of aluminum foil inside the steamer. Lay the fish flat side down on the foil in a single layer. Spread the garlic paste on top of the fish. Place the steamer tier over the boiling water and cover the steamer with its lid. Steam for 8 minutes, until the fish just begins to flake when prodded with a fork. Transfer the fish to dinner plates. Serve at once, accompanied by the lemon wedges.

Barbecued Halibut with Sweet-Sour Grapefruit Sauce

SERVES 4

6 to 8 grapefruit, unpeeled
½ cup packed brown sugar
½ cup minced green onion
1 tablespoon Asian chile sauce
½ teaspoon salt
4 (6-ounce) halibut fillets or steaks

Cut 4 of the grapefruit into ⅛-inch-thick slices. Grate the zest from 1 of the remaining grapefruit. Juice the remaining grapefruit to obtain 1 cup of juice. In a bowl, combine the grapefruit zest, grapefruit juice, sugar, green onion, chile sauce, and salt and mix well. (The grapefruit and marinade can be covered and refrigerated for up to 8 hours before using.)

Prepare a medium-hot fire in a charcoal grill or preheat a gas grill to medium (about 450°F). Place the fish in a baking dish. Stir the marinade and pour half of it over the fish, turning to coat evenly. Cover the fish and marinate in the refrigerator for 5 to 15 minutes. Lay the grapefruit slices in a tight, single layer directly on the grill rack. Place the fish on top of the grapefruit. Cover the grill and cook for 10 minutes before lifting the lid. If the fish does not flake when prodded with a fork, close the lid and cook for 2 minutes more. Transfer the fish to dinner plates and spoon the remaining marinade over. Serve at once.

Pan-Roasted Halibut with Apricots

SERVES 4

4 (6-ounce) halibut fillets
Salt and freshly ground black pepper
2 tablespoons extra virgin olive oil
½ cup dried apricots (or other dried fruit), cut into thin slices
3 tablespoons minced fresh ginger
½ cup dry white wine
2 tablespoons unsalted butter
3 tablespoons chopped fresh chives or parsley, for garnish

Preheat the oven to 450°F. Season both sides of the fish with salt and pepper.

Place a large ovenproof sauté pan over medium-high heat and add the olive oil. When the oil is hot, add the fish curved side down. Sauté for 1 minute, until the underside is lightly browned. Do not turn the fish over. Sprinkle the apricots around the sides of the fish. Sprinkle the fish with the ginger and wine. Scatter small pieces of the butter across the top of the fish.

Cover the pan and transfer to the oven. Roast for about 8 minutes, until the fish just begins to flake. Turn the fish over and transfer to dinner plates. Spoon the apricots over the fish and sprinkle with the chives. Serve at once.

Grouper, a member of the sea bass family, numbers in the hundreds of species and is found off both coasts. Some groupers weigh only 1 pound and others weigh a thousand times as much. The average size of this fish is from 5 to 15 pounds. White, flaky, moderately firm, with very low fat, some of the more popular groupers are: black, Nassau, red, yellowfin or yellowmouth, and cabrilla. Grouper can be barbecued, broiled, roasted, braised, and pan-fried.

Thai Plank-Smoked Halibut

SERVES 4

1 (4 by 12-inch) cedar or alder plank
½ cup freshly squeezed lime juice
½ cup packed brown sugar
¼ cup Thai fish sauce
1 tablespoon Asian chile sauce
¼ cup peanut, safflower, or corn oil
4 cloves garlic, minced
¼ cup chopped fresh mint
¼ cup chopped cilantro sprigs
1½ pounds halibut fillets or steaks

Submerge the plank in cold water for 8 to 24 hours. In a bowl, combine the lime juice, sugar, fish sauce, chile sauce, oil, garlic, mint, and cilantro and mix well. (The marinade can be covered and refrigerated for up to 8 hours before using.)

Prepare a medium-hot fire in a charcoal grill or preheat a gas grill to medium (about 450°F). Place the fish in a baking dish and add the marinade. Turn the fish to coat evenly. Cover and place in the refrigerator for 5 to 15 minutes. Place the plank on the grill rack. When the plank begins to smoke, place the fish flat side down on the plank. Cover the grill and cook for 15 minutes before lifting the lid. If the fish does not flake when prodded with a fork, close the lid and cook for 2 minutes more. Transfer to dinner plates and serve at once.

(Photographed at right)

Stir-Fried Orange-Hoisin Halibut

SERVES 2 TO 3

½ cup cashew nuts
1 pound halibut fillets
3 zucchini, cut into matchsticks
2 green onions, white and green parts, chopped
3 tablespoons minced fresh ginger
¼ cup freshly squeezed orange juice
2 tablespoons thin soy sauce
1 tablespoon hoisin sauce
2 teaspoons cornstarch
2 teaspoons Asian chile sauce
2 tablespoons peanut, safflower, or corn oil

Preheat the oven to 325°F. Spread the cashews on a small ungreased baking sheet and toast, stirring occasionally, for about 15 minutes, until darkened. Cut the halibut into ¼-inch-thick slices and then cut the slices into 2-inch lengths. In a bowl, combine the zucchini, green onions, and ginger (measuring no more than 4 cups in total) and toss well. In a separate bowl, combine the orange juice, soy sauce, hoisin sauce, cornstarch, and chile sauce and mix well. (The fish, vegetables, and sauce can be covered and refrigerated for up to 8 hours before using. Store the cashews at room temperature.)

Place a wok over high heat. When the wok is hot, add the oil. When the oil just begins to smoke, add the vegetables. Stir-fry for about 30 seconds, until the color brightens. Add the halibut and sauce and gently stir. Cover the wok and steam-cook for about 1 minute, until the fish flakes when prodded with a spatula. Stir and toss for about 30 seconds, until the sauce glazes the food. Transfer to dinner plates, sprinkle with the cashews, and serve at once.

ZUCCHINI MATCHSTICKS

Cut the zucchini on a diagonal into ¼-inch slices. Overlap the slices and cut into ¼-inch matchsticks.

Greek Roasted Halibut

SERVES 4

½ cup pitted imported black olives, chopped
Kernels from 2 ears of corn
½ cup chopped roasted red bell pepper
½ cup chopped fresh parsley
¼ cup extra virgin olive oil
2 tablespoons grated lemon zest
2 tablespoons minced garlic
2 teaspoons chopped fresh oregano
½ teaspoon salt
½ teaspoon freshly ground black pepper
4 (6-ounce) halibut fillets or steaks

In a bowl, combine the olives, corn, bell pepper, parsley, olive oil, lemon zest, garlic, oregano, salt, and pepper and stir well. Place the fish flat side down in a baking dish. Coat the sides and top of the fish with the marinade. (The fish can be covered and refrigerated for up to 4 hours before using.)

Preheat the oven to 400°F. Place the fish in the oven and roast for about 12 minutes, until it just begins to flake when prodded with a fork. Transfer to dinner plates and serve at once.

(Photographed at right)

Coconut Pasta with Grilled Halibut

SERVES 3 TO 4

Coconut-Curry Sauce

1 cup unsweetened coconut milk
¼ cup freshly squeezed lemon juice
2 tablespoons Chinese rice wine or dry sherry
2 tablespoons oyster sauce
1 tablespoon curry powder
1 to 3 teaspoons Asian chile sauce
2 teaspoons cornstarch
½ teaspoon sugar
¼ cup chopped cilantro sprigs or fresh basil

1½ pounds halibut fillets
2 tablespoons olive oil
Salt and freshly ground black pepper
8 ounces fusilli or other dried pasta
3 tablespoons peanut, safflower, or corn oil
2 tablespoons finely minced fresh ginger
3 green or yellow zucchini, cut into matchsticks (see page 46)

In a bowl, combine all of the ingredients for the sauce and mix well. (The sauce can be covered and refrigerated for up to 8 hours before using.)

Prepare a medium-hot fire in a charcoal grill or preheat a gas grill to medium (about 450°F). Rub the fish on both sides with the olive oil, and sprinkle with salt and pepper. Place a sheet of aluminum foil on the grill rack. Place the fish on the foil. Cover the grill and cook for 8 minutes before lifting the lid. If the fish does not flake when prodded with a fork, close the lid and cook for 2 minutes more.

Bring a large pot of water to a rapid boil over high heat. Lightly salt the water and add the pasta. Cook according to the package instructions, until al dente. Drain in a colander. Return the empty pot to the stove over high heat. Add the peanut oil and ginger and sauté for 15 seconds, until the ginger sizzles. Add the zucchini and sauce and bring to a boil. Immediately return the pasta to the pot and stir to evenly combine. Transfer the pasta to warmed dinner plates. Top each serving with a piece of the grilled fish and serve at once.

Tex-Mex Barbecued Halibut Steaks

SERVES 4

½ cup Heinz 57 Sauce
¼ cup freshly squeezed lime juice
2 tablespoons molasses
1 tablespoon minced chipotle chiles in adobo sauce
3 cloves garlic, minced
⅓ cup chopped cilantro sprigs
4 (6-ounce) halibut steaks
4 orange wedges

In a bowl, add the Heinz 57 sauce, lime juice, molasses, chipotle chiles, garlic, and half of the cilantro and mix well. (The marinade can be covered and refrigerated for up to 8 hours before using.)

Prepare a medium-hot fire in a charcoal grill or preheat a gas grill to medium (about 450°F). Place the fish in a baking dish. Stir the marinade and pour it over the fish, turning to coat evenly. Cover the fish and marinate in the refrigerator for 5 to 15 minutes. Brush the grill rack with oil. Place the fish on the rack and grill, turning once and basting with additional marinade, for about 5 minutes on each side. The fish is done when the flesh flakes easily when prodded with a fork. Transfer the fish to dinner plates. Squeeze the orange wedges over the fish, sprinkle with the remaining cilantro, and serve at once.

CHOPPING CILANTRO

The entire cilantro plant, including the stems, is used in cooking. To chop cilantro, bunch the leaves together with your fingers. Cut into thin slices and then chop.

Pan-Fried Halibut with Herbs, Olive Oil, and Soy

SERVES 4

4 (6-ounce) halibut fillets
1 tablespoon herbes de Provence, dried oregano, or dried thyme
¼ cup extra virgin olive oil
¼ cup thin soy sauce
½ teaspoon freshly ground black pepper
¼ cup unsalted butter
4 lemon wedges

Rub the halibut on both sides with the herbs, olive oil, soy sauce, and pepper.

Working in batches or using 2 large sauté pans, place the pans over medium-high heat. When hot, add the butter. When the butter begins to brown, add the fish curved side down. Pan-fry for 1 minute, until lightly browned. Turn the fish over and pan-fry for 1 minute, until the second side is lightly browned. Cover the pan and decrease the heat to low. Cook for about 5 minutes, until the fish just begins to flake when prodded with a fork. Transfer the fish to dinner plates. Squeeze the lemon wedges over the fish and serve at once.

Paper-Wrapped Halibut

SERVES 4

1 teaspoon grated lemon zest
¼ cup freshly squeezed lemon juice
¼ cup extra virgin olive oil
¼ cup chopped cilantro sprigs or fresh basil
2 tablespoons thin soy sauce
1 tablespoon brown sugar
1 teaspoon your favorite hot sauce
2 cloves garlic, minced
4 (6-ounce) halibut fillets
4 (10-inch) squares parchment paper

In a bowl, combine the lemon zest, lemon juice, olive oil, cilantro, soy sauce, brown sugar, hot sauce, and garlic and mix well. Place the fish in a baking dish. Pour the marinade over the fish and turn to coat evenly. Place in the refrigerator to marinate for 15 minutes.

Place a piece of fish on each sheet of paper. Fold the paper as shown below. Place the packages on a heavy baking sheet.

Preheat the oven to 400°F. Place the fish packages in the oven and cook for 15 minutes. Open the packages and slide the fish, seasoning, and liquid onto dinner plates. Serve at once.

PAPER-WRAPPED FISH

1) Position the paper so that a corner is pointing away from you. Place the halibut across the bottom third of the paper. 2) Fold over the bottom corner. 3) Fold over the side corner. 4) Turn the paper over. 5) Tuck the remaining corner into the envelope. 6) Crease the paper so that it stays sealed during cooking.

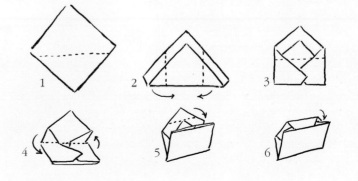

Roasted Halibut with Fruit Glaze

SERVES 4

1 cup dried apricots, sliced
1 cup dried cranberries
1 cup dried Bing cherries
3 tablespoons minced fresh ginger
2 cups white wine
¼ cup coarsely chopped fresh mint
4 (6-ounce) halibut fillets or steaks
Salt
Crushed red pepper flakes or freshly ground black pepper
1 lemon, cut into wedges

In a saucepan, combine the apricots, cranberries, cherries, ginger, 1 cup of the wine, and 2 tablespoons of the mint and mix well. Place over medium heat and bring to a simmer. Cover and cook for about 10 minutes, until the fruit softens. (The fruit can be covered and refrigerated for up to 8 hours before using.)

Preheat the oven to 350°F. Place the fish flat side down in a baking dish. Sprinkle the fish with salt and pepper flakes. Arrange the fruit on top of and around the fish. Pour the remaining 1 cup wine around the fish. Place in the oven and roast for about 12 minutes, until the fish just begins to flake when prodded with a fork. Transfer to dinner plates. Squeeze the lemon wedges over the fish. Garnish with the remaining 2 tablespoons mint and serve at once.

(Photographed at left)

Poached Halibut with Spicy Orange Sauce

SERVES 4

2 cups freshly squeezed orange juice
1½ cups water
½ cup tequila
¼ cup packed brown sugar
½ cup dried whole red chiles
5 cloves garlic, peeled and crushed
8 lime slices
1 teaspoon salt
1 teaspoon cumin seeds
1½ pounds halibut fillets
1 teaspoon grated orange zest, for garnish
1 teaspoon grated lime zest, for garnish
1 avocado, cut into 8 slices

In a saucepan or sauté pan just large enough to hold the fish, combine the orange juice, water, tequila, sugar, chiles, garlic, lime slices, salt, and cumin. Place over high heat and bring to a boil. Decrease the heat to low, cover, and simmer for 20 minutes. Add the fish, cover the pan, and turn off the heat (you can leave the pan on the burner or remove from the stove). After 10 minutes, transfer the fish to dinner plates.

Pass half of the liquid through a fine-mesh strainer into a large sauté pan. Place the pan over high heat and bring to a boil. Cook for about 5 minutes, until the sauce begins to thicken. Spoon the sauce over the fish and sprinkle the orange and lime zests over the top. Serve at once, accompanied by the avocado slices.

Chilean sea bass is not a bass at all; it is caught off the Patagonian coast and marketed in South America as "toothfish." Its sparkling white flesh and high oil content make it a wonderful-tasting fish even when badly overcooked. Unfortunately, Chilean sea bass is on the endangered list. Please do not buy this fish.

Flatfish is a large category of fish including sole, flounder, and halibut. It is so named because these fish are extremely thin and wide. Flatfish spend their lives flat against the sandy ocean floor. As they mature, their underside stays an ivory white, their upper side becomes darkly colored, and the bottom eye gradually migrates to the upper side of the head. There is a huge range of size among flatfish, from 1-pound sole to 300-pound halibut. Small flatfish are best pan-fried, while any flatfish 3 pounds or larger can be barbecued, roasted, and steamed.

Halibut Roasted in Prosciutto

SERVES 4

½ cup tapenade
2 tablespoons extra virgin olive oil
2 tablespoons chopped fresh basil
2 cloves garlic, minced
1 teaspoon grated lime zest
½ teaspoon your favorite chile sauce
½ teaspoon salt
8 (4 by 8-inch) paper-thin prosciutto slices
1½ pounds halibut fillet, cut into 8 square pieces

Preheat the oven to 450°F. In a bowl, combine the tapenade, olive oil, basil, garlic, lime zest, chile sauce, and salt and mix well. Lay the pieces of prosciutto out on a work surface. Position a piece of fish at one end of each piece of meat. Top the fish with a spoonful of the tapenade mixture. Fold the long end of the prosciutto over the fish and tuck the edges underneath.

Place the fish packages in a baking dish. Roast for 12 minutes, until the fish flakes when prodded with a fork. Transfer to dinner plates and serve at once.

(Photographed at right)

WRAPPING FISH WITH PROSCIUTTO

Place a paper-thin slice of prosciutto flat on a work surface. Position the fish at one end of the prosciutto. Top the fish with some marinade, tapenade, salsa, or pesto. Bring the long end of the prosciutto over the fish so the meat forms a single layer on top of the fish. Tuck the edges around the sides and under the fish to form a package.

Salmon

Americans eat twice as much salmon as any other fish, more than 2 pounds per capita. Meaty, flavorful, high in fat, and packed with health-enhancing omega-3 fatty acids, fresh wild salmon is the ideal fish to serve for worknight meals and parties. Each year we look forward to celebrating its season, which runs from April through early October. You can assume that all fresh salmon not labeled by supermarkets as "wild" is farm-raised.

All commercial wild salmon is fished on the Pacific Coast, with about 90 percent coming from Alaskan waters. (Wild Atlantic salmon is commercially extinct; all "Atlantic" salmon is farm raised.) There are several varieties of Pacific Coast salmon. King, or chinook, is the superior salmon, with the highest oil content and thus the richest flavor. The color is off-white to bright red. King salmon usually weigh 15 to 40 pounds, although they can reach up to 120 pounds. Kings are often named for the rivers to which they return, as with the Copper River and Yukon River salmon. Albino king salmon, which have ivory flesh and excellent flavor, are a rarity and only occasionally appear in markets. Sockeye, or red, salmon have the second highest oil content and are popular for canning. The supply, most of which comes from Alaska and Canada, peaks in July. Sockeye salmon usually weigh 5 to 15 pounds. Coho, or silver, salmon have only 60 percent of the fat of king salmon, and thus are not as flavorful. Coho flesh is paler than king or sockeye. The coho season is from July to early October, with the peak in August. Coho salmon are typically 5 to 12 pounds. Chum salmon are the lightest in color and lowest in fat. Chum weigh 8 to 10 pounds.

SUBSTITUTES:
arctic char, black cod (sablefish), black sea bass, grouper, halibut, rockfish, snapper, walleyed pike

RECOMMENDED COOKING TECHNIQUES:
barbecue, braise, broil, microwave, pan-fry, poach, roast, steam

Barbecued Salmon with Lemon-Garlic Rub

SERVES 4

2 tablespoons grated lemon zest
½ cup freshly squeezed lemon juice
⅓ cup extra virgin olive oil
⅓ cup thin soy sauce
4 cloves garlic, chopped
1 teaspoon crushed red pepper flakes
⅓ cup chopped fresh parsley
1 (1½- to 2-pound) center-cut salmon fillet, skin on,
 pin bones removed

In a bowl, combine the lemon zest, lemon juice, olive oil, soy sauce, garlic, pepper flakes, and parsley and mix well. (The rub can be covered and refrigerated for up to 8 hours before using.)

Prepare a medium-hot fire in a charcoal grill or preheat a gas grill to medium (about 450°F). Place the salmon in a baking dish. Stir the rub and pour it over the salmon, turning to coat evenly. Place in the refrigerator and marinate for 5 to 15 minutes. Place the salmon skin side down on the grill rack. Cover the grill and cook the fish for 8 minutes before lifting the lid. If the fish does not flake when prodded with a fork, close the lid and cook for 2 minutes more. Slide a spatula under the salmon (the skin will stay stuck to the grill) and transfer to a cutting board. Cut into 4 pieces, arrange on dinner plates, and serve at once.

REMOVING PIN BONES FROM SALMON

To remove the pin bones from a fillet of salmon, brush your fingers down the center of the fillet until you feel the ridge of bones. Using needle-nose pliers or fish tweezers, pull out each pin bone in the direction of the head, and try to avoid tearing the flesh.

Salmon Pasta Salad

SERVES 4

8 ounces fusilli, penne, or other dried pasta
1½ pounds salmon fillets, skinned, pin bones removed
4 cups cherry tomatoes
4 cups hothouse (English) cucumber, cut into ½-inch cubes
4 green onions, cut diagonally into ½-inch lengths
3 tablespoons wine vinegar (any type)
¼ cup thin soy sauce
1 tablespoon Asian chile sauce
2 tablespoons dark sesame oil
2 tablespoons peanut, safflower, or corn oil
2 tablespoons sugar
1 teaspoon grated orange zest
¼ cup minced fresh ginger
¼ cup chopped cilantro sprigs

Bring a large pot of water to a rapid boil. Lightly salt the water and cook the pasta according to the package instructions, until al dente. Drain in a colander, rinse with cold water, and drain thoroughly. Place the salmon in a baking dish. Position an oven rack 4 inches from the heating element and turn the oven to broil. Immediately place the salmon in the oven and cook for about 4 minutes, until it begins to flake with pressure from a fork. Allow the salmon to cool, and break into small pieces.

In a large bowl, combine the pasta, salmon, tomatoes, cucumber, and green onions and toss well. In a small bowl, combine the vinegar, soy sauce, chile sauce, sesame oil, peanut oil, sugar, orange zest, ginger, and cilantro and mix well. Pour the dressing over the pasta and toss to evenly combine. (The salad can be covered and refrigerated for up to 24 hours before using.) Gently toss the salad and serve chilled or just at room temperature.

(Photographed at right)

Barbecued Salmon Skewers

SERVES 4

1½ pounds center-cut salmon fillets, skinned,
  pin bones removed
20 (6-inch) bamboo skewers
¼ cup freshly squeezed lemon juice
¼ cup extra virgin olive oil
½ teaspoon salt
½ teaspoon freshly ground black pepper
1 recipe New Wave Tartar Sauce (optional; page 107)

Cut the salmon into strips about ¼ inch thick, 1 inch wide, and 4 inches long. Run the skewers lengthwise through the fish strips. The skewering process will be easier if you twist as you push. In a bowl, combine the lemon juice, olive oil, salt, and pepper and mix well. (The fish and marinade can be covered and refrigerated for up to 8 hours before using.)

Prepare a medium-hot fire in a charcoal grill or preheat a gas grill to medium (about 450°F). Rub the salmon skewers with the marinade. Place a strip of aluminum foil on the grill rack. Brush the rack with oil. Lay the salmon directly on the rack with the foil under (thus shielding) the exposed bamboo skewers. Grill, turning, for about 45 seconds on each side. The fish is done when it just begins to flake when prodded with a spatula. Transfer the skewers to dinner plates. Serve at once with the sauce alongside.

SKEWERING SALMON

Run the skewer through the thickest part of the fish so that the wood is only exposed at the end. Don't weave the skewer since any exposed areas will burn away.

Barbecued Salmon with Grapefruit

SERVES 4

1½ cups freshly squeezed grapefruit juice
½ cup granulated sugar
1 tablespoon cornstarch
½ teaspoon salt
1 teaspoon your favorite hot sauce
¼ cup minced fresh ginger
½ cup packed brown sugar
1 (1½-pound) center-cut salmon fillet, skinned,
  pin bones removed
4 grapefruit cut into ¼-inch slices
3 tablespoons chopped fresh chives, parsley, or cilantro sprigs

In a small saucepan, combine 1 cup of the grapefruit juice, the granulated sugar, cornstarch, salt, hot sauce, and ginger and mix well. (The sauce can be covered and refrigerated for up to 8 hours before using.)

Prepare a medium-hot fire in a charcoal grill or preheat a gas grill to medium (about 450°F). Rub the remaining ½ cup grapefruit juice and the brown sugar into the salmon flesh. Lay the grapefruit slices in a tight, single layer directly on the grill rack. Place the fish flat side down on top of the grapefruit. Cover the grill and cook the fish for 8 minutes before lifting the lid. If the fish does not flake when prodded with a fork, close the lid and cook for 2 minutes more. Transfer the salmon to a cutting board. Cut into 4 pieces and transfer to dinner plates.

Place the sauce over medium-high heat and bring to a low boil, stirring constantly for about 1 minute, until it thickens. Stir in the chives. Spoon the sauce over the salmon and serve at once.

(Photographed at right)

Stir-Fried Salmon with Asparagus

SERVES 2 TO 4

1 pound salmon fillets, skinned, pin bones removed
1 bunch asparagus
½ cup unsweetened coconut milk
2 tablespoons Thai fish sauce
1 teaspoon Asian chile sauce
1 teaspoon curry powder (optional)
1 teaspoon cornstarch
¼ cup chopped fresh basil, mint, or cilantro sprigs
2 tablespoons peanut, safflower, or corn oil
2 tablespoons minced fresh ginger
½ cup chopped green onions

Cut the salmon into ¼-inch-thick slices. Cut the slices into 1½-inch lengths. Cut the asparagus on a sharp diagonal into 1-inch lengths. In a bowl, combine the coconut milk, fish sauce, chile sauce, curry powder, cornstarch, and basil and mix well. (The fish, asparagus, and sauce can be covered and refrigerated for up to 8 hours before using.)

Place a wok over high heat. When the wok is hot, add the oil. When the oil just begins to smoke, add the asparagus, ginger, and green onions. Stir and toss for about 40 seconds, until the vegetables just begin to brighten. Stir the coconut sauce and add it to the wok. Add the salmon, stir well, and cover the wok. Cook for about 90 seconds, gently stirring every 20 seconds. When the salmon has no visible raw color, transfer to dinner plates and serve at once.

ROLL-CUTTING ASPARAGUS

Try roll-cutting asparagus for an attractive alternative to cutting asparagus on the diagonal. Make a sharp diagonal cut, then roll the asparagus a quarter turn toward you, make another sharp diagonal cut, and continue rolling and cutting, always rotating the asparagus toward you after every cut.

Smoked Salmon with Lemon Dry Rub

SERVES 6

2 tablespoons brown sugar
2 teaspoons ground cinnamon
2 teaspoons ground coriander
2 teaspoons ground cumin
1 teaspoon salt
2 teaspoons freshly ground black pepper
6 (6-ounce) center-cut salmon fillets, skinned, pin bones removed
¼ cup extra virgin olive oil
8 lemons
4 cups hickory chips or other hardwood chips, for smoking

In a bowl, combine the sugar, cinnamon, coriander, cumin, salt, and pepper and stir well. Rub the seasonings on the top and bottom of the salmon. Rub the salmon with the olive oil. Cut 7 of the lemons into ¼-inch-thick slices. Cut the remaining lemon into wedges. (The fish and lemons can be covered and refrigerated for up to 4 hours before using.)

Place the wood chips in a large bowl and fill with water to cover. Soak for 30 minutes and then drain off all water. Prepare a fire in a charcoal grill or preheat a gas grill to low (210°F to 240°F). For gas barbecues, place 2 cups of the wood chips on a sheet of aluminum foil, and place the foil on one corner of the grill rack. For charcoal barbecues, once the coals have turned ash-colored, scatter 2 cups of the wood chips across the coals.

When the chips begin to smoke, place the lemon slices in a tight, single layer directly on the grill rack. The lemon layer should be slightly larger than the size of the salmon. Place the fish flat side down in a tight layer on top of the lemons, being sure that the pieces of fish are touching. Cover the grill and maintain the heat at 210°F to 240°F. On a gas barbecue, you may need to turn off all burners except one and crack open the lid slightly. Smoke the salmon for about 30 minutes, until the flesh begins to flake when prodded with a fork. When the wood chips burn away during cooking, add the remaining 2 cups. Transfer the fish to dinner plates and serve with the lemon wedges.

Salmon, Papaya, and Avocado Salad

SERVES 4

1 cup walnuts
1 pound salmon fillets, skinned, pin bones removed
2 ripe avocados, cubed (about 2 cups)
1 firm papaya, cubed (about 2 cups)
8 cups torn salad greens
½ cup extra virgin olive oil
1 teaspoon grated lime zest
6 tablespoons freshly squeezed lime juice
2 tablespoons minced fresh ginger
½ teaspoon salt
½ teaspoon freshly ground black pepper or
   your favorite hot sauce

Preheat the oven to 325°F. Spread the walnuts on a small ungreased baking sheet and toast, stirring occasionally, for about 15 minutes, until darkened. Place the salmon in a baking dish. Position an oven rack 4 inches from the heating element and turn the oven to broil. Immediately place the salmon in the oven and cook for about 4 minutes, until it begins to flake with pressure from a fork. Allow the fish to cool to room temperature, and then break into bite-sized pieces.

In a bowl, combine the nuts, cooked salmon, avocados, papaya, and salad greens. In a small bowl, combine the olive oil, lime zest, lime juice, ginger, salt, and pepper and mix well. Add the dressing to the salad and toss to evenly combine. Transfer to dinner plates and serve at once.

ENVIRONMENTAL CONCERNS

Much has been written about environmental concerns with farm-raised salmon. Having reviewed the data, we recommend that you purchase only wild salmon. The many serious environmental issues with farm-raised salmon include: It is bio-engineered (escaped farm-raised salmon might cross with wild salmon and compromise its ability to survive in the wild). The floating feedlots are extremely harmful to surrounding fragile marine environments and communities. It takes at least 3 pounds of ground wild fish, such as herring and anchovy, to yield 1 pound of farm-raised salmon. And it is still common to add red food coloring (synthetic carotenoids) to the feed of farm-raised salmon in order to artificially color the flesh.

REMOVING SALMON SKIN

To remove the salmon skin from a center-cut fillet, cut into the tail meat or corner edge with a sharp knife. When the blade touches the skin, turn the knife at a downward angle. With the knife still facing down, cut along the skin and remove.

Broiled Salmon and Figs

SERVES 4

2 tablespoons grated lemon zest
1 cup pomegranate syrup
½ cup extra virgin olive oil
1 tablespoon your favorite hot sauce
1 tablespoon minced garlic
2 teaspoons ground cumin
⅓ cup chopped cilantro sprigs
⅓ cup chopped fresh mint
4 (6-ounce) salmon fillets (skinned, pin bones removed)
  or steaks
12 ripe figs, quartered

In a bowl, combine the lemon zest, pomegranate syrup, olive oil, hot sauce, garlic, cumin, cilantro, and mint and stir well. (The marinade can be covered and refrigerated for up to 8 hours before using.)

Position an oven rack 4 inches from the heating element. Line a baking sheet with aluminum foil. Place the salmon flat side down on the baking sheet and coat on all sides with one-third of the marinade. Scatter the figs around the fish and drizzle with half of the remaining marinade. Turn the oven to broil. Immediately place the salmon in the oven and cook for about 5 minutes, until the fish and sauce begin to caramelize. Turn the oven to bake at 300°F. Drizzle the remaining marinade over the fish and figs and cook for about 5 minutes, until the fish flakes when prodded with a fork. Transfer to dinner plates and serve at once.

(Photographed at left)

DRIED FIG VARIATION

To use dried figs instead of fresh, place the figs in a bowl and cover with boiling water. Let soak for 15 minutes. Drain well and remove the stems. Cut the figs in half to use.

Broiled Salmon with Teriyaki-Butter Glaze

SERVES 4

¼ cup teriyaki sauce
¼ cup freshly squeezed orange juice
2 tablespoons chopped fresh basil
2 tablespoons minced fresh ginger
4 (6-ounce) salmon fillets (skinned, pin bones removed)
  or steaks
2 tablespoons unsalted butter
2 teaspoons black sesame seeds, for garnish
2 teaspoons grated orange zest, for garnish
1 recipe Spicy Wasabi Sauce (page 107)

In a bowl, combine the teriyaki sauce, orange juice, basil, and ginger and mix well. (The marinade can be covered and refrigerated for up to 8 hours before using.)

Place the fish in a baking dish and add the marinade, turning to coat evenly. Place in the refrigerator to marinate for 5 to 15 minutes. Line a heavy baking dish with aluminum foil. Place the fish flat side down on the foil. Dot the top of the fish with small pieces of the butter.

Position an oven rack 4 inches from the heating element and turn the oven to broil. Immediately place the fish in the oven and cook for about 4 minutes, until golden. The flesh should flake easily when prodded with a fork. If the fish is not done, turn the oven to bake at 300°F and cook for about 2 minutes. Check again for doneness. Transfer the fish to dinner plates. Sprinkle with the sesame seeds and orange zest and serve with the sauce on the side.

Tea-Poached Salmon with Mint

SERVES 4

8 cups water
½ cup loose black tea leaves
1 cup packed mint sprigs
½ cup sugar
1 tablespoon salt
2 tablespoons Asian chile sauce
1 lemon, cut into thin slices
¼ cup chopped fresh ginger
4 (6-ounce) salmon fillets, skinned, pin bones removed
1 recipe Mango Salsa (page 107)

In a saucepan just large enough to hold the fish, combine the water, tea, mint, sugar, salt, chile sauce, lemon juice, lemon slices, and ginger over medium heat and bring to a low boil. Decrease the heat to low, cover, and simmer for 20 minutes. Add the fish. Cover the pan and turn off the heat. Let the fish sit in the tea for 20 minutes. Transfer the fish to a plate, cover, and refrigerate for at least 1 hour or up to 8 hours.

To serve, place a piece of fish on each plate. Spoon the salsa over the fish. Serve chilled or at room temperature.

Lingcod, which is found on the North American Pacific Coast, is no relation to the cod family; it is a member of the greenling family. Caught along the California coast in the summer and in Alaska during the winter, lingcod can grow up to 50 pounds. Mildly sweet tasting, firm fleshed, lowfat, and pure white, lingcod is a versatile fish that can be prepared using almost any cooking technique.

Asian Grilled Salmon Salad

SERVES 4

Dressing
¼ cup minced fresh ginger
¼ cup chopped cilantro sprigs, fresh mint, or fresh basil
½ cup freshly squeezed lime juice
½ cup packed light brown sugar
¼ cup safflower oil
3 tablespoons Thai fish sauce
1 tablespoon Asian chile sauce
1 teaspoon freshly grated nutmeg

½ cup slivered almonds
1 (1½-pound) salmon fillet, skin on, pin bones removed
2 slightly firm papaya, cut into ½-inch cubes (about 4 cups)
1 hothouse (English) cucumber, cut into ½-inch cubes (about 2 cups)
4 to 8 large Bibb lettuce leaves

Prepare a medium-hot fire in a charcoal grill or preheat a gas grill to medium (about 450°F). In a bowl, combine all of the ingredients for the dressing and stir well. Preheat the oven to 325°F. Spread the almonds on a small ungreased baking sheet and toast for about 15 minutes, until golden.

Place the salmon in a baking dish. Add half of the dressing and rub it in on both sides. Lay the salmon skin side down on the grill rack. Cover the grill and cook the fish for 8 minutes before lifting the lid. If the fish does not flake when prodded with a fork, close the lid and cook for 2 minutes more. Remove the salmon from grill using a spatula, leaving the skin on the rack. (The dressing and cooked fish can be covered and refrigerated for up to 24 hours before using. Store the almonds at room temperature.)

Break the salmon into bite-sized pieces. Place the salmon, papaya, and cucumber in a bowl. Add the remaining salad dressing and toss well. Divide the lettuce leaves among dinner plates. Spoon the salad into the center of the lettuce. Sprinkle with the almonds and serve at once.

Salmon Cakes with Dill and Ginger

SERVES 4

1½ pounds salmon fillets, skinned, pin bones removed
2 teaspoons grated lemon zest
4 teaspoons freshly squeezed lemon juice
4 teaspoons thin soy sauce
2 teaspoons chile sauce (any type)
¼ cup mayonnaise
4 teaspoons chopped fresh dill
2 tablespoons minced fresh ginger
1 cup fine unseasoned bread crumbs
3 tablespoons peanut, safflower, or corn oil
8 small butter lettuce leaves
1 recipe Aioli Dipping Sauce or Tartar Sauce (page 107)

Place the salmon on a cutting board and mince with a sharp knife. The salmon can also be minced in a food processor.

In a bowl, combine the salmon, lemon zest, lemon juice, soy sauce, chile sauce, mayonnaise, dill, and ginger and mix until evenly blended. Using your hands, form the mixture into 8 disks, each about ½ inch thick and 4 inches in diameter. Coat all sides with the bread crumbs. (The cakes can be covered and refrigerated for up to 8 hours before using.)

Working in batches or using 2 large sauté pans, place the pans over medium heat. Add the oil. When the oil is hot, add the salmon cakes. Cook, turning once, for about 1 minute on each side, until just cooked in the center (cut into one of the cakes to check for doneness). To serve, place a salmon cake in a lettuce leaf, add a spoonful of the sauce, wrap the cake, and eat.

Salmon Braised in Coconut Milk

SERVES 4

About 1 cup unsweetened coconut milk
About ⅓ cup freshly squeezed orange or tangerine juice
1 teaspoon grated orange zest
2 tablespoons Thai fish sauce
1 to 3 teaspoons Asian chile sauce
1 clove garlic, minced
2 tablespoons minced fresh ginger
2 tablespoons chopped fresh mint
2 tablespoons chopped cilantro sprigs
4 (6-ounce) salmon fillets, skinned, pin bones removed

In a saucepan just large enough to hold the fish, combine the coconut milk, orange juice, orange zest, fish sauce, chile sauce, garlic, ginger, mint, and cilantro and mix well. Add the fish and make sure it is submerged. If it is not submerged, add equal amounts of coconut milk and orange juice. Place the saucepan over medium heat and bring to a very low simmer. Cover the pan and decrease the heat to low. Cook for 6 to 8 minutes. If the fish does not flake when prodded with a fork, cover the pan and simmer for 2 minutes more. (If the fish is not submerged, turn the fish over after 5 minutes of cooking.) Gently remove the fish and place on dinner plates. Spoon the sauce around the sides and serve at once.

Arctic char, a member of the char family, is closely related to trout and salmon and has a flavor and a texture that is like a cross between the two. Arctic char can range in color from red to pale ivory. Wild char live in the icy waters (both fresh and marine) of North America and Europe. Many wild arctic char swim from the cold lakes in Canada to the ocean and then return to the point of origin to spawn. Almost all arctic char sold in markets is farm raised. It is great barbecued, broiled, roasted, steamed, pan-fried, baked, and microwaved.

Thai Steamed Salmon

SERVES 4

¼ cup dry sherry, sake, or Chinese rice wine
¼ cup freshly squeezed lime juice
2 tablespoons honey
2 tablespoons Thai fish sauce
2 tablespoons chopped fresh basil
2 tablespoons chopped fresh mint
2 tablespoons minced fresh ginger
1 serrano or jalapeño chile, minced, including seeds
4 (6-ounce) salmon fillets (skinned, pin bones removed) or steaks
¼ cup chopped roasted unsalted peanuts, for garnish
Grated zest of 1 lime, for garnish

In a bowl, combine the sherry, lime juice, honey, fish sauce, basil, mint, ginger, and chile and mix well. (The marinade can be covered and refrigerated for up to 8 hours before using. Store the peanuts at room temperature.)

Reserve 4 tablespoons of the marinade. Place the fish in a baking dish and add the remaining marinade, turning to coat evenly. Place in the refrigerator to marinate for 10 minutes. Assemble a Chinese steamer (see page 17). Bring a large saucepan or sauté pan of water to a boil over high heat. Place a sheet of aluminum foil inside the steamer. Lay the fish flat side down on the foil in a single layer. Place the steamer tier over the boiling water and cover the steamer with its lid. Steam for 8 minutes, until the fish just begins to flake when prodded with a fork. Transfer the fish to dinner plates and drizzle 1 tablespoon of the reserved marinade over each serving. Sprinkle with the peanuts and lime zest and serve at once.

(Photographed at right)

Monkfish, sometimes referred to as "poor man's lobster" (or angler fish), has a very firm, white flesh with no lobster taste whatsoever. Caught along the Atlantic Coast as far south as Brazil and as far north as the Grand Banks, this quite terrifying-looking fish can weigh up to 50 pounds. Always make sure the market has skinned the fish. Under the skin is a paper-thin purplish membrane that also needs to be removed by using your fingers or a paring knife. The very lean, lowfat flesh never flakes during cooking. Monkfish is best pan-fried, roasted, steamed, and braised.

Roasted Salmon with Herb Mayonnaise

SERVES 4

2 cloves garlic, minced
2 tablespoons shredded fresh basil
1 teaspoon grated orange zest
¼ cup mayonnaise
2 tablespoons extra virgin olive oil
1 teaspoon your favorite hot sauce
½ teaspoon salt
4 (6-ounce) salmon fillets (skinned, pin bones removed)
   or steaks
Freshly ground black pepper
1 lemon, cut into wedges

In a bowl, combine the garlic, basil, orange zest, mayonnaise, olive oil, hot sauce, and salt and mix well. (The mayonnaise can be covered and refrigerated for up to 8 hours before using.)

Preheat the oven to 300°F. Place the salmon flat side down in a baking dish. Season with salt and pepper. Spread the mayonnaise mixture evenly over the top of the salmon. Roast, uncovered, for about 18 minutes, until the salmon just begins to flake when prodded with a fork. Transfer to dinner plates. Serve at once, accompanied by the lemon wedges.

Chilled Salmon with Jade Sauce

SERVES 4

4 (6-ounce) salmon fillets, skinned, pin bones removed
2 vine-ripened tomatoes, sliced paper thin
6 inches hothouse (English) cucumber, sliced paper thin
1 recipe Jade Sauce (page 106)
2 tablespoons toasted white sesame seeds (see sidebar),
   for garnish

Preheat the oven to 300°F. Place the salmon flat side down in a baking dish and roast for 18 to 20 minutes, until it just begins to flake when prodded with a fork. Cover and refrigerate the fish for at least 1 hour and up to 8 hours.

Overlap the tomato and cucumber slices on chilled plates. Place a piece of fish on top of each serving. Stir the sauce and drizzle it on the fish. Sprinkle with the sesame seeds and serve at once.

(Photographed at right)

TOASTING SESAME SEEDS

To toast white sesame seeds, place in a dry frying pan. Place the pan over high heat. Cook for about 1 minute, stirring with a spatula to turn the sesame seeds over, until golden. Immediately remove them from the pan and allow to cool. Place in an airtight container at room temperature until ready to use. Toasted sesame seeds can also be frozen indefinitely.

Snapper

There are several hundred species of snapper, a marvelous-tasting firm-textured saltwater fish suitable for almost any cooking method. The FDA insists that only one of these species be called "red snapper" *(Lutjanus campechanus)*. Since nearly all snapper is sold filleted and skinned, it's impossible to judge whether you are buying red snapper or one of its innumerable relatives. True snapper is found throughout the world's tropical and semitropical waters. In the United States, it comes from the Caribbean and from the Virginia coast to Florida. The most common types of snapper are lane, mangrove, mutton, red, vermilion, and yellowtail. If you live on the West Coast, you'll find "red snapper," "Pacific snapper," or "rock cod" in every market. This fish is completely unrelated to snapper (or cod), and is from the rockfish family. Since these West Coast "snappers" are inferior in taste, we suggest you substitute another kind of fish if you can't find true snapper.

SUBSTITUTES:
black cod (sablefish), black sea bass, catfish, halibut, salmon (all varieties), tilapia, trout, walleyed pike

RECOMMENDED COOKING TECHNIQUES:
barbecue, braise, broil, pan-fry, roast, steam

Barbecued Snapper with Maple Syrup, Chiles, and Lemon

SERVES 4

½ cup pure maple syrup
2 tablespoons freshly squeezed lemon juice
2 tablespoons minced red or green chiles, including seeds
1 teaspoon minced garlic
½ teaspoon salt
¼ cup chopped cilantro sprigs
4 (6-ounce) snapper fillets
1 cup blueberries
½ lemon, cut into wedges

In a bowl, combine the maple syrup, lemon juice, chiles, garlic, salt, and 2 tablespoons of the cilantro and mix well. (The marinade can be covered and refrigerated for up to 8 hours before using.)

Prepare a medium-hot fire in a charcoal grill or preheat a gas grill to medium (about 450°F). Place the fish in a baking dish and rub the marinade into both sides. Place in the refrigerator to marinate for 15 minutes. Spray a sheet of aluminum foil that is slightly larger than the fish with nonstick oil or rub with oil. Place the foil on the grill rack. Place the fish on the foil. Scatter the blueberries over the fish. Cover the grill and cook the fish for 6 minutes before lifting the lid. If the fish does not flake when prodded with a fork, close the lid and cook for 2 minutes more. Transfer the fish and berries to dinner plates. Sprinkle with the remaining 2 tablespoons cilantro and a squeeze of lemon juice. Serve at once.

Steamed Snapper with Spicy Pesto

SERVES 4

8 thinly sliced pieces fresh ginger
2 cloves garlic
½ cup packed fresh basil leaves
½ cup packed cilantro sprigs
1 ounce Parmigiano-Reggiano cheese, grated (about ¼ cup)
⅓ cup toasted pine nuts (page 26)
2 teaspoons your favorite hot sauce
½ teaspoon salt
5 tablespoons extra virgin olive oil
Juice of 1 lemon
4 (6-ounce) snapper fillets

In the bowl of a food processor, combine the ginger and garlic and process until minced. Add the basil and cilantro and process until minced. Add the cheese, half of the pine nuts, the hot sauce, and the salt and process until incorporated. With the motor running, slowly add the olive oil, until a paste forms. Add the lemon juice and process just until combined. (The pesto can be covered and refrigerated for up to 8 hours before using.)

Assemble a Chinese steamer (see page 17). Bring a large saucepan or sauté pan of water to a boil over high heat. Place a sheet of aluminum foil inside the steamer. Lay the fish flat side down on the foil in a single layer. Spread the pesto evenly across the entire surface of each fillet. Place the steamer tier over the boiling water and cover the steamer with its lid. Steam for 8 minutes, until the fish just begins to flake when prodded with a fork. Transfer to dinner plates and scatter with the remaining pine nuts. Serve at once.

Pan-Fried Snapper with Shiitake Cream Sauce

SERVES 4

½ cup heavy whipping cream
¼ cup white wine
1 tablespoon minced fresh ginger
1 teaspoon dark sesame oil
½ teaspoon grated orange zest
½ teaspoon salt
¼ teaspoon freshly ground black pepper
4 (6-ounce) snapper fillets
¼ cup all-purpose flour
3 tablespoons peanut, safflower, or corn oil
3 tablespoons unsalted butter
¼ pound fresh shiitake mushrooms, stemmed and
  cut into ⅛-inch strips
¼ cup chopped fresh parsley, for garnish

In a bowl, combine the cream, wine, ginger, sesame oil, orange zest, salt, and pepper and mix well. Sprinkle both sides of the fish with salt and pepper and dust with the flour, shaking off all excess. (The sauce and fish can be covered and refrigerated for up to 8 hours before using.)

Working in batches or using 2 large sauté pans, place the pans over medium-high heat. When the pans are hot, divide 1½ tablespoons of the oil and 1½ tablespoons of the butter between the 2 pans. When the butter is lightly browned, place the fish curved side down in the pan. Cook for about 1 minute, until lightly browned. Turn the fish over, cover the pan, and decrease the heat to low. Cook for about 5 minutes, until the fish just begins to flake when prodded with a fork. Transfer the fish to dinner plates.

Return 1 of the pans to the stove over high heat. Add the remaining 1½ tablespoons oil and 1½ tablespoons butter. When the butter melts, add the mushrooms. Sauté for 30 seconds, then add the cream sauce. Bring to a boil and cook for 1 minute, until the sauce thickens and turns light brown. Spoon the sauce over the fish, sprinkle with the parsley, and serve at once.

Broiled Snapper with Peaches and Grapes

SERVES 4

4 (6-ounce) snapper fillets
Salt and freshly ground black pepper
¼ cup unsalted butter
2 tablespoons chopped fresh tarragon or other herbs
2 cloves garlic, minced
2 small peaches or nectarines, peeled and sliced
2 cups red table grapes, halved
¼ cup slivered almonds, for garnish

Line a heavy baking dish with aluminum foil. Rub the fish on both sides with salt and pepper. Place the fish flat side down in the baking dish. In a small saucepan over medium-high heat, melt the butter. Stir in the tarragon and garlic, and then pour evenly over the fish. Scatter the peaches and grapes around the fish.

Position an oven rack 4 inches from the heating element and turn the oven to broil. Immediately place the fish in the oven and cook for about 4 minutes, until golden. The flesh should flake easily when prodded with a fork. If the fish is not done, turn the oven to bake at 300˚F and cook for 1 minute. Check again for doneness. Transfer to dinner plates, sprinkle with the almonds, and serve at once.

(Photographed at right)

Tilapia is one of the most widely available farm-raised fish. Although it can grow to 3 pounds, most tilapia is harvested at about 1½ pounds and then filleted before being shipped to markets. Examine the fish carefully before buying to make sure it has not been frozen. Its delicate, lowfat, white flesh and slightly soft texture are ruined by freezing. Tilapia should be pan-fried or broiled.

Walleyed pike, sometimes called yellow pike, is not actually related to pike; it is a type of perch. An extremely popular Midwestern fish, the fish is farm raised in the Great Lakes region and harvested in the 1- to 2-pound range. With white, mild-tasting flesh and a slightly firm texture, this is a versatile fish. Substitute walleyed pike for any of the trout, catfish, black cod, halibut, or salmon recipes in this book. It is great barbecued, broiled, roasted, pan-fried, and steamed.

Stove-Top Smoked Snapper

SERVES 2

¼ cup freshly squeezed lime juice
¼ cup honey
¼ cup extra virgin olive oil or nut oil
1 tablespoon your favorite hot sauce
1 teaspoon ground cumin
1 teaspoon salt
2 cloves garlic, minced
¼ cup chopped fresh chives, basil, mint, or cilantro sprigs
2 (6-ounce) snapper fillets

In a bowl, combine the lime juice, honey, oil, hot sauce, cumin, salt, garlic, and chives and stir well. (The marinade can be covered and refrigerated for up to 8 hours before using.)

Place the fish in a baking dish and rub with half of the marinade. Place in the refrigerator to marinate for 5 to 15 minutes, and reserve the remaining marinade. Place the stove-top smoker over medium-high heat. Add 2 tablespoons of wood chips in an even layer on the bottom of the smoker. Place the fish on the wire rack and insert the wire rack into the smoker. Cover the smoker tightly. Cook for 12 minutes, until the fish just begins to flake easily when prodded with a fork. Transfer to dinner plates. Spoon the remaining marinade over the fish and serve at once.

STOVE-TOP SMOKER

Stove-top smokers don't actually smoke fish, but they are great for imparting a delicate smoky taste to the exterior of the fish. Stove-top smokers, which are sold at most cookware shops, typically include packages of various powdered wood chips. All you need to do is sprinkle 2 tablespoons of wood chips on the bottom of the smoker, wait until the wood begins to smoke, place the fish inside, and cover. Adding more than 2 tablespoons of wood chips will not increase the intensity of the smoke flavor. Stove-top smokers are not only convenient and easy to use, but they are tightly sealed and your kitchen will not fill with smoke. This recipe works well with East Coast snapper, or you can use catfish, lingcod, or black cod. West Coast rockfish (sold as snapper or rock cod) has too coarse a flesh for this preparation.

Pan-Fried Tangerine Snapper

SERVES 4

¼ cup sliced almonds
3 tablespoons chopped fresh tarragon, basil, or mint
2 teaspoons grated tangerine zest
Juice of 4 tangerines (1 cup)
2 tangerines, peeled and segmented
4 teaspoons brown sugar
½ teaspoon salt
4 (6-ounce) snapper fillets
Salt and freshly ground black pepper
3 tablespoons unsalted butter
3 small cloves garlic, minced

Preheat the oven to 325°F. Spread the almonds on a small ungreased baking sheet and toast for about 10 minutes, until golden. In a bowl, combine the tarragon, tangerine zest, tangerine juice, tangerine segments, sugar, and salt, and mix well. (The sauce can be covered and refrigerated for up to 8 hours before using. Store the almonds at room temperature.)

Preheat the oven to 400°F. Sprinkle both sides of the fish with salt and pepper. Place 2 large ovenproof sauté pans over medium-high heat. When hot, add the butter and garlic. When the butter melts, add the fish, curved side down. Cook for about 1 minute, until lightly browned. Turn the fish over and transfer the pans to the oven. Cook for about 8 minutes, until the fish just begins to flake when prodded with a fork. Transfer the fish to dinner plates.

Return 1 of the sauté pans to the stove over high heat. Add the sauce and bring to a boil. Boil for 2 minutes, until thickened. Pour the sauce over the fish. Garnish with the almonds and serve at once.

New Orleans-Style Blackened Snapper

SERVES 2

2 cloves garlic, minced
2 (6-ounce) snapper fillets
½ teaspoon dried thyme
½ teaspoon dried oregano
½ teaspoon ground cayenne pepper
¼ teaspoon salt
½ teaspoon freshly ground black pepper
¼ teaspoon paprika
2 tablespoons extra virgin olive oil
1 lemon, cut into wedges

Rub the garlic on both sides of the fish. Combine the thyme, oregano, cayenne, salt, pepper, and paprika and mix well. Rub the spices on both sides of the fish and then rub the fish with the olive oil. (The fish can be covered and refrigerated for up to 8 hours before using.)

Place a large cast-iron skillet over high heat. Heat for about 15 minutes, until the surface of the pan turns a duller color. Add the fish to the pan, curved side down. Give the pan a shake so the fish does not stick. Cook for 90 seconds. Turn off the heat and turn the fish over. Cook for about 3 minutes, until the fish just begins to flake. Transfer the fish to dinner plates, accompanied by the lemon wedges.

ABOUT BLACKENED FISH

Blackened fish, popularized by New Orleans–based chef Paul Prudhomme, is typically made with redfish, also known as red drum. Blackened redfish became so popular in the 1980s that red drum were nearly fished out of Gulf Coast waters. Fresh snapper or any other fish listed on page 70 works fine for this dish. It's essential to use a cast-iron frying pan preheated over high heat until the metal turns a duller color, about 15 minutes. We depart from orthodoxy by blackening the fish on just one side and then turning it over and completing the cooking with the heat turned off.

Green Thai-Curried Snapper

SERVES 4

4 cloves garlic
2 tablespoons sliced fresh ginger
1 cup packed basil leaves, mint leaves, or cilantro sprigs
1 teaspoon ground coriander
1 teaspoon caraway seeds
1 teaspoon ground cumin
1/2 cup peanut, safflower, or corn oil
2/3 cup unsweetened coconut milk
2 tablespoons Thai fish sauce
4 (6-ounce) snapper fillets
Asian chile sauce, for garnish
1 lime, cut into wedges

In the bowl of a food processor, combine the garlic and ginger and process until minced. Add the basil and process until minced. Add the coriander, caraway, and cumin and process until incorporated. With the motor running, slowly add 3 to 4 tablespoons of the oil, until a paste forms. Transfer the paste to a bowl, add the coconut milk and fish sauce, and stir well. (The sauce can be covered and refrigerated for up to 8 hours before using.)

Working in batches or using 2 large sauté pans, place the pans over medium heat. When the pans are hot, add the remaining 1/4 cup oil. When the oil is hot, add the fish, curved side down. Cook, turning once, for about 1 minute on each side, until lightly browned. Pour in the sauce. Cover the pans and decrease the heat to low. Simmer for 5 minutes, until the fish just begins to flake when prodded with a fork. Transfer the fish to dinner plates. Spoon the sauce over the top. Garnish with dots or splashes of the chile sauce and serve with the lime wedges.

(Photographed at left)

Pan-Fried Snapper with Lemon Sauce

SERVES 4

2 teaspoons grated lemon zest
1/2 cup freshly squeezed lemon juice
6 tablespoons sugar
1/4 cup white wine
2 teaspoons cornstarch
1 teaspoon your favorite hot sauce
1/2 teaspoon salt
1 clove garlic, finely minced
4 (6-ounce) snapper fillets
Salt and freshly ground black pepper
1/4 cup all-purpose flour
2 tablespoons peanut, safflower, or corn oil
2 tablespoons unsalted butter
2 tablespoons chopped fresh chives, parsley, mint, or cilantro sprigs, for garnish

In a bowl, combine the lemon zest, lemon juice, sugar, wine, cornstarch, hot sauce, salt, and garlic and mix well. Sprinkle both sides of the fish with salt and pepper and dust with the flour, shaking off all excess. (The sauce and fish can be covered and refrigerated for up to 8 hours before using.)

Working in batches or using 2 large sauté pans, place the pans over medium-high heat. When the pans are hot, add the oil and butter. When the butter is lightly browned, place the fish curved side down in the pan. Cook for about 1 minute, until lightly browned. Turn the fish over, cover the pan, and decrease the heat to low. Cook for about 5 minutes, until the fish just begins to flake when prodded with a fork. Transfer the fish to dinner plates.

Wipe out the oil from 1 of the sauté pans and return it to the stove over high heat. Stir the lemon sauce and add it to the pan. Bring to a boil and immediately pour over the fish. Sprinkle the fish with the chives and serve at once.

Sole

 Sole is part of a vast family of flatfish (including halibut and flounder) that spends its life resting flat, half buried in sand, on the ocean floor. It is white on the underside and darker on the top and, like all flatfish, as the fish matures, the eye looking at the sand gradually migrates to the upper side of the head. The only true sole sold along America's eastern seaboard is Dover sole, imported from Europe. Dover sole is virtually unattainable in most of the country; much of what is sold as Dover sole is actually flounder. But there are many flatfish that work well as substitutes, including lemon sole and gray sole, caught in the Atlantic, and petrale sole, from the California coast. Lemon sole and gray sole are firm enough to barbecue, broil, and pan-fry. Petrale sole is fragile; it's best cooked briefly in a hot, heavy frying pan.

SUBSTITUTES:
butterfish, catfish, freshwater bass, rockfish, sea trout, snapper, tilapia, walleyed pike, whiting

RECOMMENDED COOKING TECHNIQUES:
barbecue, broil, pan-fry

Barbecued Lemon Sole with Apricot and Lime

SERVES 4

3 tablespoons chopped fresh mint or basil
2 cloves garlic, finely minced
1 tablespoon minced fresh ginger
1/3 cup freshly squeezed lime juice
1/4 cup apricot jam
3 tablespoons peanut, safflower, or corn oil
1 to 3 teaspoons your favorite hot sauce
1/2 teaspoon salt
4 (6-ounce) lemon or gray sole fillets

In a bowl, combine the mint, garlic, ginger, lime juice, jam, oil, hot sauce, and salt and stir well. (The marinade can be covered and refrigerated for up to 8 hours before using.)

Prepare a medium-hot fire in a charcoal grill or preheat a gas grill to medium (about 450°F). Place the fish in a baking dish and add the marinade, turning to coat evenly. Place in the refrigerator to marinate for 5 to 15 minutes. Spray a sheet of aluminum foil that is slightly larger than the fish with nonstick oil or rub with oil. Place the foil on the grill rack and place the fish on the foil. Cover the grill and cook for 5 minutes before lifting the lid. If the fish does not flake when prodded with a fork, close the lid and cook for 2 minutes more. Transfer the fish to dinner plates and serve at once.

Orange roughy, caught off the coast of New Zealand, is usually a disappointment. It's often frozen on ship, then thawed and filleted on shore before being refrozen and shipped to other countries. The quality is unreliable, so we do not recommend buying orange roughy.

Pan-Fried Sole with Tomato-Lemon Sauce

SERVES 4

½ cup chopped tomatoes (fresh, bottled, or boxed)
¼ cup chopped fresh basil
2 teaspoons grated lemon zest, plus extra for garnish
2 teaspoons your favorite hot sauce
½ teaspoon salt
1½ pounds equal-size sole fillets
Freshly ground black pepper
¼ cup all-purpose flour
¼ cup extra virgin olive oil
2 tablespoons unsalted butter
4 cloves garlic, chopped

In a bowl, combine the tomatoes, basil, lemon zest, hot sauce, and salt and mix well. (The sauce can be covered and refrigerated for up to 8 hours before using.)

Working in batches or using 2 sauté pans, place the pans over medium-high heat. Sprinkle salt and pepper on both sides of the fish. Lightly coat the fish on both sides with the flour, shaking off all excess. Add the olive oil and butter to the pans. When the butter begins to brown, add the sole, curved side down, in a single layer. Cook, turning once, for 30 to 60 seconds on each side. The fish is done when it flakes easily when prodded with a spatula. Transfer the fish to dinner plates.

Return 1 of the pans to the stove over medium-high heat. Add the garlic and sauté for 15 seconds, then add the sauce. Bring to a rapid boil and remove the pan from the heat. Spoon the sauce around the fish, garnish with grated lemon zest, and serve at once.

(Photographed at left)

Pan-Fried Sole with Wilted Spinach

SERVES 4

4 cups gently packed spinach leaves (about 4 ounces)
1 large clove garlic, minced
2 dried red chiles
1 tablespoon thin soy sauce
1 teaspoon dark sesame oil
½ teaspoon sugar
Salt and freshly ground black pepper
4 (6-ounce) lemon or gray sole fillets
¼ cup all-purpose flour
¼ cup plus 2 tablespoons peanut, safflower, or corn oil

In a large bowl, combine the spinach, garlic, chiles, soy sauce, sesame oil, and sugar and toss until evenly coated. Sprinkle salt and pepper on both sides of the fish and dust with the flour, shaking off all excess.

Working in batches or using 2 large sauté pans, place the pans over medium-high heat. When the pans are hot, add the ¼ cup oil. When the oil is hot, add the sole curved side down in a single layer. Cook, turning once, for about 1 minute on each side. The sole is done when it flakes easily when prodded with a spatula. Transfer the fish to dinner plates.

Return 1 of the pans to the stove over high heat and add the 2 tablespoons oil. When the oil just begins to smoke, add the spinach. Using tongs or a spatula, rapidly toss the spinach. The moment the spinach wilts, but has not begun to release its moisture, spoon it over the fish and serve at once.

Pan-Fried Sole with Toasted Almonds

SERVES 4

⅓ cup sliced almonds
4 (6-ounce) lemon or gray sole fillets
½ teaspoon salt
½ teaspoon freshly ground black pepper
¼ cup all-purpose flour
2 tablespoons peanut, safflower, or corn oil
3 tablespoons unsalted butter
1 shallot, minced
1 clove garlic, minced
½ cup white wine
2 tablespoons chopped fresh parsley, for garnish
4 lemon wedges

Preheat the oven to 325°F. Spread the almonds on a small ungreased baking sheet and toast for about 10 minutes, until golden. Sprinkle the fish on both sides with ¼ teaspoon of the salt and ¼ teaspoon of the pepper. Dust the fish on both sides with the flour, shaking off all excess.

Working in batches or using 2 large sauté pans, place the pans over medium-high heat. When the pans are hot, add the oil. When the oil is hot, add the fish curved side down in a single layer. Cook, turning once, for about 1 minute on each side. The sole is done when it flakes easily when prodded with a spatula. Transfer the fish to dinner plates.

Return 1 of the pans to the stove over medium-high heat and add the butter. When the butter melts, add the shallot and garlic. Cook for about 30 seconds, until the shallot is transparent. Add the wine, the remaining ¼ teaspoon salt, and the remaining ¼ teaspoon pepper. Cook for about 20 seconds, until the wine begins to thicken. Add the almonds and sauté for 5 seconds. Spoon the sauce over the sole and sprinkle with the parsley. Serve at once, accompanied by the lemon wedges.

Pan-Fried Sole with Brown Butter

SERVES 4

Salt and freshly ground black pepper
1½ pounds equal-size sole fillets
¼ cup all-purpose flour
¼ cup unsalted butter, cut into 4 pieces
¼ cup chopped fresh parsley, or 2 tablespoons chopped fresh chives, cilantro sprigs, or basil, for garnish
1 lemon, cut into wedges

Sprinkle salt and pepper on both sides of the fish. Working in batches or using 2 sauté pans, place the pans over medium-high heat. Lightly coat the sole on both sides with the flour, shaking off all excess. Place the butter in the pans. When the butter browns slightly, add the sole, curved side down, in a single layer. Cook, turning once, for 30 to 60 seconds on each side. The sole is cooked when it just begins to flake when prodded with a spatula. Transfer to dinner plates and sprinkle with the parsley. Serve accompanied by lemon wedges.

COOKING PETRALE SOLE

Petrale sole will brown better if it is cooked in a cast-iron skillet (for even heat distribution) with butter rather than oil. Heat the pan over medium-high heat and then add the butter in small pieces and let it brown slightly before adding the fillets. The cooking takes so little time that everything accompanying the fish should already be on the dinner plates.

Broiled Lemon Sole with Mushrooms

SERVES 4

1 cup chicken broth
3 tablespoons oyster sauce
1 tablespoon dark sesame oil
½ teaspoon sugar
½ teaspoon freshly ground black pepper
¼ cup olive oil
½ pound button, cremini, or shiitake mushrooms, thinly sliced
½ cup chopped green onions, fresh parsley, or chives
4 (6-ounce) lemon or gray sole fillets
Salt
¼ cup chopped fresh chives or parsley, for garnish

In a bowl, combine the broth, oyster sauce, sesame oil, sugar, and pepper and mix well. Place a sauté pan over medium heat and add the olive oil. When the oil is hot, add the mushrooms and green onions. Sauté for about 5 minutes, until the mushrooms begin to wilt. Add the broth mixture and bring to a boil for about 3 minutes, until the sauce begins to thicken. Remove from the heat and allow to cool. (The sauce can be covered and refrigerated for up to 8 hours before using.)

Position an oven rack 4 inches from the heating element. Sprinkle both sides of the fish with salt and pepper. Place the fish flat side down in a heavy baking dish. Spoon the sauce over the fish. Turn the oven to broil. Immediately place the pan in the oven and cook for about 5 minutes, until the fish begins to flake when prodded with a fork. Transfer the fish to dinner plates. Sprinkle with the chives and serve at once.

Potato-Crusted Sole with Spicy Ketchup

SERVES 4

4 cups potato chips
1 teaspoon ground cayenne pepper
1½ pounds equal-size sole fillets
¼ cup all-purpose flour
3 eggs, well beaten
¼ cup unsalted butter, cut into 4 pieces
1 lemon, cut into wedges
1 recipe Spicy Ketchup (page 108)

Place the chips in the bowl of a food processor and process until finely ground (you will have about 1 cup). Transfer to a bowl and stir in the cayenne. Lightly coat the sole on both sides with the flour, shaking off all excess. Dip the fish in the eggs, then coat on both sides with the ground chips. (The battered fish can be covered and refrigerated for up to 8 hours before using.)

Working in batches or using 2 sauté pans, place the pans over medium-high heat. When hot, add the butter. When the butter begins to brown, add the sole, curved side down, in a single layer. Cook, turning once, for 30 to 60 seconds on each side. The sole is done when it just begins to flake when prodded with a spatula. Transfer to dinner plates. Serve with the lemon wedges and ketchup.

Blackfish is a popular sport fish on both the Pacific and Atlantic Coasts. In California, one acclaimed species is called sheepshead. Blackfish has very white, firm flesh and a low fat content, and its sweet taste may be due to its diet of shellfish. It has a delicious, delicate flavor. Don't confuse blackfish with a boney freshwater fish by the same name. Blackfish is also called Chinese steelhead and black trout. Blackfish is great barbecued, broiled, pan-fried, and steamed.

Swordfish

 Swordfish is a magnificent creature, swimming throughout the oceans of the world, weighing up to 1,000 pounds, and pointing its way with a fearsome bony sword that makes up one-third of its length. Because East Coast swordfish is an endangered species, buy swordfish caught off the California coast or from the deep Pacific waters near the Hawaiian Islands. Flawlessly fresh swordfish has firm, dense, meatlike flesh that is white to strikingly pink with a small red blood line coursing through the edge of the steaks. Always buy fresh swordfish (frozen and thawed swordfish is a taste catastrophe) that is at least 1 inch thick. Look for evenly cut swordfish steaks. Last, it's always better to cook a large swordfish steak and then cut it into serving-sized pieces than to portion it prior to cooking—the fish will be moister with less surface area exposed to heat.

SUBSTITUTES:
black cod (sablefish), lingcod, mahi mahi, ono, opah, salmon (all varieties), shark, sturgeon, yellowtail

RECOMMENDED COOKING TECHNIQUES:
barbecue, broil, pan-fry, roast

Swordfish Tacos with Mango Salsa

SERVES 4

1½ pounds (1-inch-thick) swordfish steaks
Salt and freshly ground black pepper
¼ cup extra virgin olive oil
8 (8-inch) flour tortillas
2 tablespoons unsalted butter
6 cups shredded iceberg lettuce
1 recipe Mango Salsa (page 107)

Prepare a medium-hot fire in a charcoal grill or preheat a gas grill to medium (about 450°F). Sprinkle both sides of the swordfish with salt and pepper and rub with the olive oil.

Brush the grill rack with oil. Place the fish on the rack and grill, turning once, for about 2 minutes on each side, until it is lightly browned and marked by the grill rack. Decrease the heat to low and move the fish to the edge of the grill, away from direct heat. Close the barbecue and cook, turning several times, for another 4 to 6 minutes, recovering the barbecue each time. The heat should be maintained at 300°F. The fish is done when it has just lost its raw color in the center.

Place the tortillas on the barbecue and cook, turning once, for about 45 seconds on each side, until lightly charred. Remove the tortillas from the grill, rub one side with a little butter.

Place some of the lettuce in each tortilla. Slice the swordfish and divide among the tortillas. Spoon on the salsa and serve at once.

TO TRIM OR NOT?

Some markets trim away the blood line, making it more difficult to quickly judge the freshness of the fish (the blood line should not be brown). Since the blood line is slightly richer tasting, we prefer to leave it alone and let dinner guests make their own gastronomic decisions.

Cantonese Stir-Fried Swordfish

SERVES 2 TO 3

1 pound swordfish, skinned
¼ cup chopped green onions
¼ cup dry sherry or Chinese rice wine
¼ cup tomato sauce
3 tablespoons oyster sauce
½ teaspoon Asian chile sauce
1 tablespoon dark sesame oil
2 teaspoons cornstarch
2 tablespoons peanut, safflower, or corn oil
2 tablespoons minced fresh ginger

Cut the swordfish into ¼-inch-thick slices and cut the slices into 2-inch lengths. In a bowl, combine the green onions, sherry, tomato sauce, oyster sauce, chile sauce, sesame oil, and cornstarch and mix well. (The fish and the sauce can be covered and refrigerated for up to 8 hours before using.)

Place a wok over high heat. When the wok is hot, add the oil and ginger. When the oil just begins to smoke, add the swordfish. Stir-fry for about 30 seconds, until the swordfish loses its raw outside color. Pour in the sauce. Stir and toss for about 1 minute, until the sauce glazes the fish. Transfer to dinner plates and serve at once.

Sturgeon, once plentiful in the wild, have been known to grow to the prodigious size of 30 feet long and 4,000 pounds! Now a 30-pound sturgeon is considered large. Wild sturgeon are caught in the spring and fall, but most sturgeon sold in markets are farm raised. Sturgeon are very firm, white-fleshed, low in fat, and have a delicate flavor. Because it is so lean, it quickly becomes dry if overcooked. Sturgeon is best barbecued, broiled, and pan-fried.

Grilled Swordfish Salad with Blue Cheese-Bacon Dressing

SERVES 4

Blue Cheese–Bacon Dressing
8 lean bacon strips
2 cloves garlic, minced
1/3 cup extra virgin olive oil or any nut oil
1/3 cup freshly squeezed orange juice
1/2 teaspoon salt
1/2 teaspoon freshly ground black pepper or
    your favorite hot sauce
1/2 cup blue cheese, crumbled

1/2 cup walnuts
1 1/2 pounds (1-inch-thick) swordfish steaks
2 tablespoons olive oil
Juice of 1 lemon or lime
1/2 teaspoon salt
8 cups torn salad greens
3 vine-ripened tomatoes, cut into 6 slices each

To prepare the dressing, in a small frying pan, cook the bacon over low heat for about 4 minutes, until crisp. Remove the bacon from the pan and drain on paper towels until cool. When cool enough to handle, crumble the bacon. In a bowl, combine half of the bacon, the garlic, oil, orange juice, salt, pepper, and cheese and mix well.

Preheat the oven to 325°F. Spread the walnuts on a small ungreased baking sheet and toast, stirring occasionally, for about 15 minutes, until darkened. Cut the fish into long strips about 1/3 inch thick. (The dressing and fish can be covered and refrigerated for up to 8 hours before using. Store the walnuts at room temperature.)

Prepare a medium-hot fire in a charcoal grill or preheat a gas grill to medium (about 450°F). Rub the fish with the olive oil, lemon juice, and salt. Brush the grill rack with oil. Place the fish on the rack and grill, turning, for about 2 minutes, until it just begins to flake.

Place the greens and tomatoes in a bowl, add the dressing, and toss to evenly coat. Divide the salad among dinner plates. Top each serving with the fish. Sprinkle with the walnuts and the remaining bacon and serve at once.

(Photographed at right)

Chinese Barbecued Swordfish

SERVES 4

¼ cup hoisin sauce
2 tablespoons oyster sauce
2 tablespoons plum sauce
2 teaspoons Asian chile sauce
¼ cup freshly squeezed lemon juice
1 tablespoon minced fresh ginger
2 cloves garlic, chopped
1½ to 2 pounds (1-inch-thick) swordfish steaks

In a bowl, combine the hoisin sauce, oyster sauce, plum sauce, chile sauce, lemon juice, ginger, and garlic and stir well. (The marinade can be covered and refrigerated for up to 8 hours before using.)

Prepare a medium-hot fire in a charcoal grill or preheat a gas grill to medium (about 450°F). Place the fish in a baking dish and add the marinade, turning and rubbing to coat evenly. Place in the refrigerator to marinate for 15 minutes. Brush the grill rack with oil. Place the fish on the rack and grill, tuning once, for about 2 minutes on each side, until it is lightly browned and marked by the grill rack. Decrease the heat to low and move the fish to the edge of the grill, away from direct heat. Close the barbecue and cook, turning several times, for another 4 to 6 minutes, recovering the barbecue each time. The heat should be maintained at 300°F. The fish is done when it has just lost its raw color in the center. Transfer the swordfish to dinner plates and serve at once.

Opah, also called "moonfish" because of its moonlike shape, is one of the most colorful of the commercial fish species available in Hawaii. Ranging in size from 60 to 200 pounds, it often swims in the company of tuna. With its rich, full flavor, firm texture, and light pink color, it is a good substitute for swordfish. Opah can be barbecued, broiled, roasted, and pan-fried.

Pan-Roasted Swordfish with Caramelized Onions

SERVES 4

6 tablespoons extra virgin olive oil
2 yellow onions, thinly sliced
¼ cup balsamic vinegar
3 cloves garlic, minced
1½ pounds (1-inch-thick) swordfish steaks
½ teaspoon salt
½ teaspoon freshly ground black pepper
1 cup roasted red bell pepper, thinly sliced
¼ cup chopped fresh parsley, for garnish

Place a large sauté pan over medium heat and add 3 tablespoons of the olive oil. When the oil is hot, add the onions. Sauté for 2 minutes, until the onions begin to sizzle. Decrease the heat to low, add the balsamic vinegar, and cook, turning occasionally, for about 15 minutes, until the onions become golden. Add the garlic and cook for 1 minute. (The onions can be covered and refrigerated for up to 8 hours before using.)

Preheat the oven to 300°F. Rub the fish with the salt and pepper on both sides. Place 2 ovenproof sauté pans over medium-high heat. Add the remaining 3 tablespoons olive oil to the pans. When the oil is hot, add the fish. Cook, turning once, for about 1 minute on each side, until the fish is light golden. Scatter the caramelized onions and the bell pepper over the fish. Place the pans in the oven and cook for about 5 minutes, until the fish just loses its raw interior color. Transfer to dinner plates. Sprinkle with the parsley and serve at once.

Broiled Swordfish with Compound Butters

SERVES 4

1 recipe Lemon-Ginger, Mint-Basil, or Chipotle-Lime
   Compound Butter (page 108)
1½ pounds (1-inch-thick) swordfish steaks

Rub half of the butter in an even layer on 1 side of the fish. (The fish can be covered and refrigerated for up to 8 hours before using.)

Position an oven rack 4 inches from the heating element. Line a baking dish with aluminum foil. Place the fish butter side up on the foil. Turn the oven to broil. Immediately place the fish butter side up in the oven and cook for about 4 minutes, until it begins to brown. The flesh should flake easily when prodded with a fork. If the fish is not done, turn the oven to bake at 300°F and cook for about 2 minutes. Check again for doneness. Rub the top side of the fish with the remaining butter during the last minute of cooking. Transfer the fish to dinner plates and serve at once.

Shark is a wonderful fish with firm, sweet flesh and a low fat content. It's a very lean fish, dense and meatlike, so care should be taken not to overcook it or it will taste dry. The two most popular varieties are mako and thresher shark. Shark is best prepared like swordfish—barbecued, broiled, roasted, and pan-fried.

Swordfish-Mushroom Pasta

SERVES 3 TO 4

½ cup heavy whipping cream
¼ cup chicken broth
½ teaspoon salt
½ teaspoon freshly ground black pepper
½ teaspoon sugar
8 ounces dried fusilli, bow ties, or other dried pasta
¼ cup unsalted butter
4 cloves garlic, chopped
½ pound button, cremini, or shiitake mushrooms, thinly sliced
1½ pounds (1-inch-thick) swordfish steaks, cut into
   bite-sized pieces
1 ounce Parmigiano-Reggiano cheese, grated (about ¼ cup)
½ cup chopped fresh parsley, for garnish

In a bowl, combine the cream, broth, salt, pepper, and sugar and mix well. (The sauce can be covered and refrigerated for up to 8 hours before using.)

Bring a large pot of water to a rapid boil. Lightly salt the water and cook the pasta according to the package instructions, until al dente. Drain in a colander. Return the empty pot to the stove over high heat. Add the butter and garlic. When the butter melts, add the mushrooms. Sauté for about 4 minutes, until the mushrooms lose their volume. Add the sauce and bring to a rapid boil. Return the pasta to the pot and add the fish. Stir for about 3 minutes, until the fish turns white and is cooked through. Stir in the cheese. Transfer to dinner plates. Sprinkle with the parsley and serve at once.

Barbecued Swordfish with Chiles and Garlic

SERVES 4

1 tablespoon grated lime zest
¼ cup freshly squeezed lime juice
¼ cup extra virgin olive oil
¼ cup packed brown sugar
¼ cup chopped cilantro sprigs
½ teaspoon salt
2 serrano chiles, minced, including seeds, or
   1 tablespoon your favorite hot sauce
2 large cloves garlic, minced
1½ pounds (1-inch-thick) swordfish steaks

In a bowl, combine the lime zest, lime juice, olive oil, sugar, cilantro, salt, chiles, and garlic and mix well. (The marinade can be covered and refrigerated for up to 8 hours before using.)

Place the fish in a baking dish and add the marinade, turning to coat evenly. Place in the refrigerator to marinate for 15 minutes.

Prepare a medium-hot fire in a charcoal grill or preheat a gas grill to medium (about 450°F). Brush the grill rack with oil. Place the fish on the rack and grill, tuning once, for about 2 minutes on each side, until it is lightly browned and marked by the grill rack. Decrease the heat to low and move the fish to the edge of the grill, away from direct heat. Close the barbecue and cook, turning several times, for another 4 to 6 minutes, recovering the barbecue each time. The heat should be maintained at 300°F. The fish is done when it has just lost its raw color in the center. Transfer the swordfish to dinner plates and serve at once.

(Photographed at left)

ABOUT GRILLING SWORDFISH

Perfectly grilled swordfish steaks require careful management of the heat. If you let the heat get too high (over 325°F), the interior of the swordfish will be dry. For best results, once the swordfish has become lightly colored on both sides, move the steaks away from the direct heat (this is called indirect cooking), and close the barbecue. Maintain the heat in the 300°F range, turning the swordfish steaks every 1 to 2 minutes. The steak surface should be beautifully browned but still wet and the interior should be moist. If you're using swordfish cut into strips, grill over medium heat. Grilled swordfish strips are delicious not only on salads but rolled inside charred flour tortillas, placed in pita bread pockets along with salsa and shredded lettuce, or added on top of pasta dishes.

Trout

Trout is one of life's great gastronomic pleasures. Today there is good-quality farm-raised rainbow trout available in many markets. Weighing 10 to 16 ounces, they range in color from white to salmon, depending on what they have been fed. When buying trout, choose fish with crystal-clear eyes, bright red gills, and skin with a beautiful iridescent sheen from a transparent, slippery layer of moisture. Trout scales are so tiny that it's unnecessary to scale them, or for that matter to wash perfectly fresh trout. (If it needs to be washed, don't buy it!) Given a choice between boned and bone-in trout, purchase the latter. Bone-in trout has a firmer texture and more flavor, and it deteriorates less during shipping and storage. It's also unnecessary to remove the head. The head is beautiful, and the checks are delicious. Trout fillets will work well in any of the following recipes in place of the whole trout. Just ask the market to fillet the trout.

SUBSTITUTES (filleted or whole, weighing no more than 1½ pounds):
bluefish, catfish, coho salmon, freshwater bass, pompano, rockfish, snapper, walleyed pike

RECOMMENDED COOKING TECHNIQUES:
barbecue, braise, pan-fry, poach, roast, steam

Barbecued Trout with Grilled Figs

SERVES 4

1 tablespoon grated orange zest
1 tablespoon grated lemon zest
½ cup freshly squeezed lemon juice
¼ cup honey
¼ cup chopped fresh basil, mint, parsley, or
   cilantro sprigs, or a combination
2 tablespoons minced fresh ginger
1 tablespoon your favorite chile sauce
½ teaspoon salt
16 ripe figs, quartered
4 (8- to 12-ounce) whole trout, bone-in or boned

In a bowl, combine the orange zest, lemon zest, lemon juice, honey, basil, ginger, chile sauce, and salt and mix well. If the trout has not been boned, diagonally slash the fish 4 times on each side. (The marinade and the fish can be covered and refrigerated for up to 8 hours before using.)

Prepare a medium-hot fire in a charcoal grill or preheat a gas grill to medium (about 450°F). Stir the marinade and add the figs. Stir well. Place the fish in a baking dish. Rub the marinade into both sides of the fish, including into the slashes and cavities. Spray a sheet of aluminum foil that is slightly larger than the fish with nonstick oil or rub with oil. Lay the foil on the grill rack. Place the trout side by side on the foil. Lay the figs on the foil next to the trout. Cover the grill and cook the fish, turning once, for 5 minutes on each side, until the flesh just begins to flake when prodded with a fork. Transfer the fish and figs to dinner plates and serve at once.

Pan-Fried Trout in Spicy Lemon Sauce

SERVES 4

2 tablespoons grated lemon zest
1 cup freshly squeezed lemon juice
½ cup chicken broth
½ cup sugar
¼ cup thin soy sauce
2 tablespoons minced serrano chile, including seeds
2 tablespoons minced fresh ginger
½ teaspoon salt
4 (8- to 12-ounce) whole trout, bone-in or boned
Freshly ground black pepper
½ cup cornstarch
¼ cup peanut, safflower, or corn oil
½ cup chopped green onions
2 tablespoons toasted white sesame seeds (page 68),
   for garnish

In a bowl, combine the lemon zest, lemon juice, broth, sugar, soy sauce, chile, ginger, and salt and mix well. (The sauce can be covered and refrigerated for up to 8 hours before using.)

Place a large sauté pan over medium-high heat. Sprinkle the fish with salt and pepper on both sides and inside the cavities. Rub cornstarch on both sides of the trout, and inside the cavities. Add the oil to the hot pan, and when the oil is hot, add the trout. Regulate the heat so that the oil is always sizzling but not smoking. Cook, turning once, for about 2 minutes on each side, until golden. Transfer the trout to a plate.

Wipe out the pan and return to high heat. Add the sauce and bring to a boil. Return the trout to the pan and add the green onions. Turn the trout over, coating it on all sides with the sauce, and cook for about 2 minutes, until the trout begins to flake when prodded with a fork. Transfer to dinner plates. Sprinkle with the sesame seeds and serve at once.

Braised Trout with Olive-Garlic Pesto

SERVES 4

½ cup imported pitted black olives
½ cup packed basil leaves
6 tablespoons extra virgin olive oil
1 teaspoon your favorite hot sauce
¼ teaspoon salt
4 cloves garlic, chopped
4 (8- to 12-ounce) whole trout, bone-in or boned
2 vine-ripened tomatoes, thinly sliced
Freshly ground black pepper

Preheat the oven to 450°F. In a food processor, combine the olives, basil, 3 tablespoons of the olive oil, hot sauce, salt, and garlic and process into a paste. Diagonally slash the fish 4 times on each side. Fill the slashes with the pesto.

Cover the bottom of a heavy baking dish with the tomato slices. Place the trout on top of the tomatoes. Brush the trout with the remaining 3 tablespoons olive oil and sprinkle with salt and pepper.

Place the baking dish in the oven and roast uncovered for about 10 minutes, until the fish begins to flake when prodded with a fork. Transfer the trout and tomatoes to dinner plates and serve at once.

Barbecued Trout with Marmalade and Chiles

SERVES 4

¼ cup orange marmalade
¼ cup thin soy sauce
2 tablespoons freshly squeezed lime juice
1 tablespoon minced serrano or jalapeño chile, including seeds
2 cloves garlic, minced
1 tablespoon minced fresh ginger
½ teaspoon salt
4 (8- to 12-ounce) whole trout, bone-in or boned
Grated zest of 1 lime, for garnish

In a bowl, combine the marmalade, soy sauce, lime juice, chile, garlic, ginger, and salt and mix well. If the trout has not been boned, diagonally slash the fish 4 times on each side. (The marinade and the fish can be covered and refrigerated for up to 8 hours before using.)

Prepare a medium-hot fire in a charcoal grill or preheat a gas grill to medium (about 450°F). Stir the marinade. Place the fish in a baking dish. Rub the marinade into both sides of the fish, including the slashes and cavities. Spray a sheet of aluminum foil that is slightly larger than the fish with nonstick oil or rub with oil. Lay the foil on the grill rack. Lay the trout on the foil. Cover the grill and cook the fish, turning once, for 5 minutes on each side, until the flesh just begins to flake when prodded with a fork. Transfer the fish to dinner plates, sprinkle with the lime zest, and serve at once.

(Photographed at right)

The **striped bass** you'll find in markets is a cross between wild striped bass and a freshwater species called white bass. Farm raised, it weighs 1 to 10 pounds. Its mild flavor, moderately firm flesh, and moderate fat content make it a very popular restaurant dish and a good choice for home cooks to barbecue, broil, roast, pan-fry, poach, and steam.

Roasted Trout with Raisins, Chiles, and Cinnamon

SERVES 4

2 teaspoons grated orange zest
1 cup freshly squeezed orange juice
¼ cup honey
2 teaspoons your favorite hot sauce
1 teaspoon ground cinnamon
½ teaspoon salt
½ cup dark raisins
4 cloves garlic, minced
¼ cup chopped cilantro sprigs
4 (8- to 12-ounce) whole trout, bone-in or boned

In a bowl, combine the orange zest, orange juice, honey, hot sauce, cinnamon, salt, raisins, garlic, and cilantro and mix well. (The marinade can be covered and refrigerated for up to 8 hours before using.)

Preheat the oven to 450°F. Stir the marinade. Place the trout flat side down in a baking dish just large enough to hold the fish. Rub the marinade into both sides of the fish, including the cavities. Roast for about 15 minutes, until the fish just begins to flake when prodded with a fork. Transfer the fish to dinner plates. Spoon the accumulated sauce over the fish and serve at once.

Pompano is a member of the jack family. Pompano is caught off the South Atlantic and Gulf states. It's a small fish weighing up to about 3 pounds. White, firm, succulent flesh with a moderate fat content and mild, delicate flavor, it is best barbecued, broiled, and pan-fried.

Pan-Fried Trout Fillets

SERVES 4

3 cloves garlic, minced
2 tablespoons minced fresh ginger
2 tablespoons minced fresh basil
2 tablespoons minced green onion
2 tablespoons toasted white sesame seeds (page 68)
½ teaspoon crushed red pepper flakes
½ teaspoon salt
4 (8- to 12-ounce) whole trout, filleted (skin on)
¼ cup extra virgin olive oil
¼ cup unsalted butter
4 lemon wedges

In a bowl, combine the garlic, ginger, basil, green onion, sesame seeds, pepper flakes, and salt and mix well. (The rub can be covered and refrigerated for up to 8 hours before using.)

Rub the trout fillets with the olive oil, and then spread with the rub. Working in batches or using 2 large sauté pans, place the pans over medium-high heat. Add 1 tablespoon of the butter to the pan. When the butter begins to brown, add the trout skin side up. Pan-fry for 2 minutes, adjusting the heat so that the trout is always sizzling in the pan. Turn the trout over and cook for 2 minutes, until the flesh just begins to flake when prodded with a fork. Transfer the trout skin side down to dinner plates.

Return 1 of the sauté pans to the stove over medium-high heat. Add the remaining 2 tablespoons butter and swirl until melted. Pour the butter over the trout and serve at once, accompanied by the lemon wedges.

(Photographed at right)

Tuna

Tuna is becoming one of America's most popular fish. Perhaps it's the very firm flesh, the immense size, the super-freezing process, or the very high fat content, but neither the flavor nor the texture of these huge deepwater fish is compromised by freezing. Tuna ranges in color from pink to bright red. Often the steaks have a blackish section of flesh, which has a more intense flavor and can be ignored or cut off, depending on personal preference. The belly meat is preferable, since its higher fat content provides more flavor and tenderness. There are several species of tuna sold in markets. We suggest you buy only ahi (bigeye) and bluefin tuna. These are the most prized because of the firm texture, deep red flesh, and high fat content. The lighter colored and lower fat yellowfin tuna doesn't have as unctuous a flavor. Tuna is best served charred on the outside but raw to medium rare in the center. Cooked beyond this point, it acquires a terrible, dry consistency. If you prefer fully cooked fish, then substitute one of the choices listed below.

SUBSTITUTES (fully cooked):
black drum, lingcod, ono, opah, shark, sturgeon, swordfish, yellowtail

RECOMMENDED COOKING TECHNIQUES:
barbecue, broil, pan-fry

Seared Tuna Salad

SERVES 4

1½ pounds (1-inch-thick) ahi or bluefin tuna steaks
¾ cup extra virgin olive oil or any nut oil
¼ cup balsamic vinegar
1 tablespoon honey
1 tablespoon mayonnaise
1 teaspoon your favorite hot sauce
½ teaspoon salt
1 clove garlic, chopped
1 red onion, halved
Freshly ground black pepper
8 cups baby lettuce greens, or torn mixed lettuce leaves
⅔ cup imported black olives, pitted and halved
1 (12-ounce) jar water-packed quartered artichoke hearts,
    drained and patted dry

Cut the tuna into long strips, each about ½ inch thick. In a blender, combine 6 tablespoons of the oil, the vinegar, honey, mayonnaise, hot sauce, salt, and garlic, and process for 5 seconds. (The fish and the dressing can be covered and refrigerated for up to 8 hours before using.)

Prepare a very hot fire in a charcoal grill or preheat a gas grill to high (about 600°F). Brush the tuna and the onion with the remaining 6 tablespoons oil and sprinkle with salt and pepper. Place the tuna on the grill rack and sear, turning, for a total cooking time of about 30 seconds. The tuna should be charred on the outside and raw to rare in the center. Place the onion on the rack and grill for about 2 minutes, until lightly charred. Remove the onion from the grill and chop into bite-sized pieces.

In a large bowl, combine the onion, lettuce, olives, and artichoke hearts. Add the dressing and toss to evenly coat. Divide the salad among dinner plates. Top each serving with equal portions of the tuna and serve at once.

Grilled Tuna Skewers with Chipotle Rub

SERVES 4

1½ pounds (1-inch-thick) ahi or bluefin tuna steaks
20 to 26 (6-inch) bamboo skewers
½ cup freshly squeezed lime juice
¼ cup packed brown sugar
¼ cup extra virgin olive oil
3 cloves garlic, minced
1 tablespoon minced chipotle chiles in adobo sauce
½ teaspoon ground cumin
½ teaspoon salt
¼ cup chopped cilantro sprigs

Cut the fish into ¼-inch-wide and 4-inch-long strips. Using a twisting motion, run a skewer lengthwise through a strip of fish so that the tip of the skewer is barely visible. Repeat with the remaining fish and skewers. In a bowl, combine the lime juice, sugar, olive oil, garlic, chiles, cumin, salt, and cilantro and mix well. (The marinade can be covered and refrigerated for up to 8 hours before using.)

Prepare a very hot fire in a charcoal grill or preheat a gas grill to high (about 600°F). Rub the tuna skewers with the marinade. Place a strip of aluminum foil on the grill rack. Brush the rack with oil. Lay the tuna directly on the rack with the foil under the exposed bamboo skewers to shield them. Grill, turning, for a total cooking time of about 30 seconds. The tuna should be charred on the outside and raw to rare in the center. Transfer to dinner plates and serve at once.

Grilled Peppered Tuna

SERVES 4

1½ pounds (1-inch-thick) ahi or bluefin tuna steaks
½ teaspoon salt
2 tablespoons freshly ground black pepper
3 tablespoons extra virgin olive oil
1 tablespoon grated lemon zest
1 tablespoon grated orange zest, plus extra for garnish
1 recipe New Wave Tartar Sauce (page 107)

Cut the tuna into 1-inch-wide strips to form 1-inch cubes. Rub the tuna on all sides with the salt, pepper, olive oil, lemon zest, and orange zest. Prepare a very hot fire in a charcoal grill or preheat a gas grill to high (about 600°F). Brush the grill rack with oil and immediately place the tuna on the rack. Sear for 15 seconds on each of the 4 sides, for a total cooking time of 1 minute. The tuna should be charred on the outside and raw to rare in the center. Transfer to dinner plates and sprinkle with grated orange zest. Serve at once, accompanied by the tartar sauce.

(Photographed at left)

CUTTING TUNA

Tuna is cut into 1-inch-square strips to provide a greater ratio of seared exterior to raw to medium rare interior. The searing must be done over very high heat to prevent the interior from becoming overcooked.

Caesar Salad with Grilled Tuna

SERVES 4

Caesar Dressing
¼ cup freshly squeezed lemon juice
¼ cup extra virgin olive oil
2 tablespoons honey
1 tablespoon dark sesame oil
1 tablespoon mayonnaise
2 teaspoons Asian chile sauce
½ teaspoon salt
2 cloves garlic, chopped
¼ cup loosely packed cilantro sprigs or basil leaves

1½ pounds (1-inch-thick) ahi or bluefin tuna steaks
¼ cup extra virgin olive oil
Salt and freshly ground black pepper
8 cups torn hearts of romaine lettuce
1 to 2 cups homemade or store-bought croutons
½ cup grated Parmigiano-Reggiano cheese

In a blender, combine all of the dressing ingredients and process until thoroughly mixed. Prepare a very hot fire in a charcoal grill or preheat a gas grill to high (about 600°F). Cut the tuna into long strips, each about ½ inch thick. Rub the tuna with the olive oil, salt, and pepper. Brush the grill rack with oil and immediately add the tuna. Sear, turning, for a total cooking time of about 30 seconds. The tuna should be charred on the outside and raw to rare in the center. Transfer the tuna to a plate. (The dressing and fish can be covered and refrigerated for up to 8 hours before using.)

In a large bowl, combine the lettuce and the dressing and toss to evenly coat. Add the croutons and cheese and toss gently. Divide the salad among dinner plates. Top each serving with equal portions of the tuna and serve at once.

Asian Grilled Tuna

SERVES 4

¼ cup wasabi powder
¼ cup thin soy sauce
¼ cup freshly squeezed lime or lemon juice
¼ cup toasted white sesame seeds (page 68)
1½ pounds (1-inch-thick) ahi or bluefin tuna steaks
Lime or lemon wedges

In a small bowl, combine the wasabi powder, soy sauce, lime juice, and sesame seeds and mix well. Cut the tuna into 1-inch-wide strips as shown on page 101. (The marinade and fish can be covered and refrigerated for up to 8 hours before using.)

Prepare a very hot fire in a charcoal grill or preheat a gas grill to high (about 600°F). Rub the tuna on all sides with the marinade. Brush the grill rack with oil and immediately place the tuna on the rack. Sear for 15 seconds on each of the 4 sides, for a total cooking time of 1 minute. The tuna should be charred on the outside and raw to rare in the center. Transfer to dinner plates and serve at once, accompanied by lime wedges.

Mahi mahi, or dolphinfish, has no relation to mammalian dolphin. Mahi mahi can be found in the warm waters around the world, and is fished along the Atlantic Coast, particularly off Florida, along the Pacific from California to South America, and in Hawaiian waters. Mahi mahi ranges in weight from 3 to 50 pounds and can be purchased in fillets and steaks. It's a moderately fat, firm, flavorful fish with off-white flesh. The fillets have a strip of brown running down the center that does not have a distinctive taste and thus does not have to be cut away. Mahi mahi is best barbecued, pan-fried, roasted, and braised.

Wok-Seared Tuna in Flour Tortillas

SERVES 2

1 pound (1-inch-thick) ahi or bluefin tuna steaks
2 tablespoons oyster sauce
1 tablespoon hoisin sauce
2 teaspoons Asian chile sauce
1 tablespoon dark sesame oil
2 tablespoons minced fresh ginger
4 (8-inch) flour tortillas
1 tablespoon unsalted butter
2 tablespoons peanut, safflower, or corn oil
2 cups shredded iceberg lettuce
½ cup cilantro sprigs

Cut the tuna into ¼-inch-wide and 2-inch-long slices. In a bowl, combine the oyster sauce, hoisin sauce, chile sauce, sesame oil, and ginger and mix well. (The fish and the marinade can be covered and refrigerated for up to 8 hours before using.)

In a bowl, combine the fish and the marinade and gently toss to coat evenly. Lightly char both sides of the tortillas on a gas burner, gas barbecue, or in a cast-iron skillet over high heat. Rub the top surface of the tortillas with the butter.

Place a wok over high heat. When the wok is very hot, add the oil. When the oil begins to smoke, add the fish. Stir and toss constantly for about 1 minute, until the fish loses its raw outside color. Transfer the fish to a platter. To serve, assemble the fish, lettuce, and cilantro in the tortillas. Roll up and eat.

(Photographed at right)

Spicy Tuna Cakes

SERVES 4

1½ pounds ahi or bluefin tuna steak, minced
2 serrano chiles, minced, including seeds
¼ cup chopped fresh mint or cilantro sprigs
¼ cup mayonnaise
2 tablespoons oyster sauce
2 teaspoons minced garlic
2 teaspoons grated orange zest
1 cup crushed panko bread crumbs
2 tablespoons peanut, safflower, or corn oil
4 to 8 mango slices or avocado slices
1 recipe Aioli Dipping Sauce (page 107)

In a bowl, combine the tuna, chiles, mint, mayonnaise, oyster sauce, garlic, and orange zest. Using your fingers, gently mix until evenly blended. Form the tuna into 4 equal balls, and then flatten gently with your palm. Coat on all sides with the bread crumbs. (The cakes can be covered and refrigerated for up to 8 hours before using.)

Place a sauté pan over medium-high heat and add the oil. When the oil begins to smoke, add the cakes. Fry, turning once, for about 30 seconds on each side, until the exterior is browned and the interior is still raw to rare. Serve at once, accompanied by the mango slices and the sauce.

Seared Tuna Burger with Wasabi Sauce

SERVES 4

2 (¾-pound, 1-inch-thick) ahi or bluefin tuna steaks
¼ cup toasted white sesame seeds (page 68)
2 tablespoons thin soy sauce
2 teaspoons dark sesame oil
4 hamburger buns, toasted
1 recipe Spicy Wasabi Sauce (page 107)
12 thin slices ripe mango or papaya
Lettuce leaves

Cut each piece of tuna in half horizontally to produce four ½-inch-thick steaks. Sprinkle both sides with the sesame seeds, soy sauce, and sesame oil.

Prepare a very hot fire in a charcoal grill or preheat a gas grill to high (about 600°F). Alternatively, heat a cast-iron skillet over high heat. Brush oil on the grill rack or in the skillet and add the tuna. Cook, turning once, for about 10 seconds on each side. The tuna should be charred on the outside and raw to rare in the center. Assemble the tuna on the buns with the sauce, mango slices, and lettuce, and serve at once.

(Photographed at right)

Ono (the Hawaiian word meaning "good to eat" or "sweet"), or wahoo, is the most delicate tasting of all fish in the mackerel family. Its flavor is often compared to albacore. Weighing up to 100 pounds, but normally caught in the 20- to 40-pound range, this is a firm, low-fat fish whose very pale pink slightly sweet flesh turns white when cooked. It is delicious barbecued, broiled, and pan-fried.

Tartar Sauces, Salsas, and Relishes

In this chapter, we've collected some of our favorite flavor accents for fish. You'll notice that we don't specify a type of fish or a cooking method to accompany these sauces. We've found that they all work equally well with any fish or cooking technique. The sauces come in the most handy when you're improvising a simple dish. One night the combination might be grilled swordfish seasoned with salt, pepper, and olive oil and accompanied by Caper-Dill Sauce; another night a pan-fried fillet of sole might be accented with Mexican Salsa. Experiment and add some extra flavor to your next dish.

Spicy Cocktail Dip

MAKES 1 CUP

1 cup store-bought taco sauce
Juice of 1 lime
1 teaspoon or more your favorite hot sauce
2 tablespoons chopped cilantro sprigs
1 clove garlic, finely minced

In a bowl, combine all of the ingredients and mix well. Cover and refrigerate. The dip will keep for up to 3 days only. Use on broiled, barbecued, or battered fish.

Spicy Thai Banana Salsa

MAKES 2 CUPS

3 half-green bananas, peeled
2 tablespoons chopped cilantro sprigs
1 tablespoon finely minced fresh ginger
3 tablespoons freshly squeezed lime juice
2 tablespoons light brown sugar
2 tablespoons Thai or Vietnamese fish sauce
2 teaspoons Thai or other Asian chile sauce

Cut the bananas lengthwise into quarters and then cut crosswise into $1/8$-inch-wide pieces. In a bowl, combine all of the ingredients and mix well. Cover and refrigerate. The salsa should be used the day it is made. Use on broiled, barbecued, or battered fish.

Jade Sauce

MAKES 1½ CUPS

2 cups packed spinach leaves
¼ cup cilantro sprigs
8 basil leaves
2 cloves garlic, chopped
1 tablespoon chopped fresh ginger
1 tablespoon grated lemon zest
2 teaspoons grated orange zest
3 tablespoons freshly squeezed lemon juice
½ cup freshly squeezed orange juice
2 tablespoons thin soy sauce
2 tablespoons sugar
1 tablespoon dark sesame oil
1 tablespoon Asian chile sauce

Combine all of the ingredients in a blender and process until smooth. Cover and refrigerate. The sauce should be used the day it is made. Use on barbecued, broiled, or roasted fish.

New Wave Tartar Sauce

MAKES ¾ CUP

½ cup mayonnaise
1 tablespoon freshly squeezed lemon or lime juice
1 teaspoon Grand Marnier
½ teaspoon Worcestershire sauce
½ teaspoon your favorite hot sauce
¼ teaspoon salt
½ teaspoon grated orange zest
1 tablespoon finely minced fresh ginger
1 tablespoon chopped cilantro sprigs

In a bowl, combine all of the ingredients and mix well. Cover and refrigerate. The sauce will keep for up to 1 week. Use on pan-fried, broiled, barbecued, or battered fish.

Tartar Sauce

MAKES ¾ CUP

½ cup mayonnaise
2 tablespoons freshly squeezed lemon or lime juice
1 tablespoon chopped fresh dill, tarragon, or parsley
¼ cup chopped sweet or dill pickles
¼ teaspoon salt
½ teaspoon your favorite hot sauce or freshly ground black pepper

In a bowl, combine all of the ingredients and mix well. Cover and refrigerate. The sauce will keep for up to 1 week. Use on pan-fried, broiled, barbecued, or battered fish.

Mango Salsa

MAKES 1½ CUPS

2 tablespoons minced green onion
2 tablespoons chopped cilantro sprigs
1 tablespoon finely minced fresh ginger
1 large mango or papaya, chopped (1 cup)
3 tablespoons freshly squeezed lime juice
2 tablespoons light brown sugar
½ teaspoon salt
2 teaspoons your favorite hot sauce

In a bowl, combine all of the ingredients and mix well. Cover and refrigerate. The salsa will keep for 12 hours. Use on broiled, barbecued, or battered fish.

Spicy Wasabi Sauce

MAKES ¾ CUP

½ cup mayonnaise
3 tablespoons wasabi powder
2 tablespoons freshly squeezed lemon or lime juice
1 tablespoon finely minced fresh ginger
¼ teaspoon salt

In a bowl, combine the mayonnaise and wasabi powder, stirring until the wasabi is absorbed. Add the lemon juice, ginger, and salt and mix well. Cover and refrigerate. The sauce will keep for up to 1 week. Use on pan-fried, broiled, barbecued, or battered fish.

Aioli Dipping Sauce

MAKES 1½ CUPS

1 cup mayonnaise
1 (7-ounce) jar roasted red bell pepper, drained and minced
4 cloves garlic, finely minced
2 teaspoons freshly squeezed lemon juice
Pinch of freshly ground white pepper

In a bowl, combine all of the ingredients and mix well. Cover and refrigerate. The sauce will keep for up to 4 days. Use on broiled, barbecued, or battered fish.

Mexican Salsa

MAKES 1½ CUPS

3 vine-ripened tomatoes, chopped (1 cup)
¼ cup chopped cilantro sprigs
1 green onion, white and green parts, chopped
1 serrano or jalapeño chile, minced, including seeds
2 tablespoons tequila
2 tablespoons freshly squeezed lime juice
2 tablespoons spicy tomato juice
½ teaspoon salt

In a bowl, combine all of the ingredients and mix well. Cover and keep at room temperature. The salsa should be used on the day it is made. Use on broiled, barbecued, or battered fish.

Guacamole

MAKES 1½ CUPS

2 ripe avocados, mashed
2 tablespoons minced green onions
1 tablespoon minced cilantro sprigs
½ teaspoon finely minced garlic
1 tablespoon freshly squeezed lemon juice
1 teaspoon your favorite hot sauce
¼ teaspoon salt

In a bowl, combine all of the ingredients and mix well. Cover tightly with plastic wrap, pressing it against the surface of the guacamole. Refrigerate until chilled. The guacamole will keep for up to 12 hours.

Caper-Dill Sauce

MAKES ¾ CUP

½ cup mayonnaise
2 tablespoons capers in brine, rinsed and drained
2 tablespoons freshly squeezed lemon juice
1 tablespoon chopped fresh dill, basil, or mint
¼ teaspoon salt
¼ teaspoon freshly ground black pepper or
    your favorite hot sauce

In a bowl, combine all of the ingredients and mix well. Cover and refrigerate. The sauce will keep for up to 1 week. Use on pan-fried, broiled, barbecued, or battered fish.

Lemon-Ginger Compound Butter

MAKES ¾ CUP

2 tablespoons minced fresh ginger
2 tablespoons grated lemon zest
½ teaspoon Asian chile sauce
¼ teaspoon salt
½ cup unsalted butter, at room temperature

In the bowl of a food processor, combine the ginger, lemon zest, chile sauce, and salt, and process until finely minced. Add the butter and process until evenly blended. Cover and refrigerate. The butter will keep for up to 1 week in the refrigerator, or indefinitely in the freezer. Use on roasted, broiled, barbecued, or pan-fried fish.

Chipotle-Lime Compound Butter

MAKES ¾ CUP

1 tablespoon minced chipotle chiles in adobo sauce
1 tablespoon grated lime zest
2 cloves garlic, minced
¼ teaspoon salt
½ cup unsalted butter, at room temperature

In the bowl of a food processor, combine the chiles, lime zest, garlic, and salt, and process until finely minced. Add the butter and process until evenly blended. Cover and refrigerate. The butter will keep for up to 1 week in the refrigerator, or indefinitely in the freezer. Use on roasted, broiled, barbecued, or pan-fried fish.

Mint-Basil Compound Butter

MAKES ¾ CUP

3 cloves garlic, minced
¼ cup packed basil leaves
¼ cup packed mint leaves
¼ teaspoon salt
½ teaspoon freshly ground black pepper
½ cup unsalted butter, at room temperature

In the bowl of a food processor, combine the garlic, basil, mint, salt, and pepper and process until finely minced. Add the butter and process until evenly blended. Cover and refrigerate. The butter will keep for up to 1 week in the refrigerator, or indefinitely in the freezer. Use on roasted, broiled, barbecued, or pan-fried fish.

COMPOUND BUTTERS

A tablespoon or so of a compund butter should be placed on top of the fish just before it comes off the grill or out of the oven. The butter will melt quickly and infuse the fish with a nice additional flavor. Compound butter can also be used in place of plain butter for sautéing.

Spicy Ketchup

MAKES ½ CUP

½ cup ketchup
1 teaspoon Asian chile sauce
2 teaspoons freshly squeezed lime juice
1 teaspoon grated fresh ginger

In a bowl, combine all of the ingredients and mix well. Cover and refrigerate. The ketchup will keep for up to 1 week. Use on broiled, barbecued, or battered fish.

Acknowledgments

Many friends helped bring this book into print and we are deeply appreciative of your support and many contributions. Thank you Ten Speed Press, particularly Phil Wood; our publisher, Lorena Jones; and Jo Ann Deck and Dennis Hayes in special sales. Many thanks also to our editor Holly Taines White, who did a wonderful job molding the book into its final form. And a special thanks to Hugh's assistant Patricia Landis, for her help throughout the project. Our friend and book designer, Beverly Wilson, contributed her unique vision and added so much to our pleasure working on this book. Food stylist Carol Cole worked on many of the photos, and added her culinary and artistic skills to the photography. Sharon Chew spent many hours working by our sides testing recipes. Lastly, several authorities helped us better understand the vast subject of fish: thank you to Mike Skladany, Roger Berkowitz, Harold McGee, Fred Howard, and Linda Saunto.

After the recipes were tested at our home and used in cooking classes, the following home cooks gave a final evaluation. This book gained much from their insights. Thank you Eleanor Altman, Kathleen Bergin, Bob Boll, Judy Bonzi, Brooke Bower, Buki Burke, Geri and Larry Campbell, Sheila Canzian, Pamela Cincola, Kris Cox, Debbie Crowther, Steve and Dara Davey, Elizabeth Eaton, Judy Farquar, Suzanne Figi, Connie Firring, Fran Folsom, Colin and Diane Forkner, Janie and Ron Frazar, Sharie and Ron Goldfarb, Margaret Healey, Mary and Valarie Huff, Linda and Ron Johnson, Lynn and Bruce Kaplan, Candy and Gil Katen, Bettylu Kessler, Walter Kinney and Kathy Mason, Terry and Irene Koch, Susan Krueger, Patricia Landis, Diana and Richard Langston, Jean Limpert, Karen Lippold and Peter Siegel, Kevin and Paula Maguire, Shelly Massey, Norma Meyer, Joan and Ed Nahikian, Connie Nyhan, Susan Olson-Schoenbaum, Jo Raphael, Joe and Karen Redden, Cambria Scalapino, Christine Stalder, David Taylor, Bob and Judy Torrie, Jonathon and Glenna Valley, Peggy Wooster, and Karen Young.

Artist Credits

Most of the tablewares in this book are from our favorite store, Vanderbilts Gallery in St. Helena, Napa Valley. Charles Gautreaux of Vanderbilts represents a wide range of ceramic artists in Italy, France, and the United States. For this book, we loved the look of the hand-painted plates from Deruta and Radda, Chianti, Italy. Also the Italian Vietri line, with its vivid colors, made many of these photos come alive. Sebastopol, California, ceramic artist Aletha Soule made many of the beautiful solid color plates, which pair so well with the Italian wares. Thanks to Mary, Marilyn, and Uta for all your help. For the cover and opening page, we chose the black and white inscribed ceramics of the ever-talented Kathy Erteman of New York City. Thank you all for being part of this book.

Index

A

Aioli Dipping Sauce, 107
Almonds, Toasted, Pan-Fried Sole
    with, 82
Apricots
    Barbecued Lemon Sole with Apricot
      and Lime, 79
    Pan-Roasted Halibut with, 44
Arctic char, 65
Asparagus
    roll-cutting, 60
    Stir-Fried Salmon with, 60
Avocados
    Guacamole, 108
    Salmon, Papaya, and Avocado
      Salad, 61

B

Banana Salsa, Spicy Thai, 106
Barbecuing, 13–14
Barbecuing-roasting, 14
Bass
    Chilean sea, 51
    striped, 94
Black Cod, 24
    Barbecued Black Cod Tostados, 32
    Barbecued Coconut-Pineapple Black
      Cod, 25
    Broiled Black Cod with Vanilla,
      Butter, and Walnuts, 29
    Pan-Fried Black Cod with Salsa, 28
    Pan-Fried Black Cod with Tomatoes
      and Olives, 25
    Pan-Roasted Black Cod with
      Andouille Sausage, 28
    Pan-Roasted Black Cod with Herb
      Rub, 26
    Pine Nut-Crusted Black Cod, 26
    Plank-Smoked Black Cod with Dill
      and Ginger, 31
    Poached Black Cod with Lemon-Dill
      Mayonnaise, 29
    Roasted Black Cod with Indian
      Spices, 31
Blackened fish, 75
Blackfish, 83
Broiling, 15
Burger, Seared Tuna, with Wasabi
    Sauce, 104
Butter(s), 20
    compound, 89, 108

C

Capers, 20
    Caper-Dill Sauce, 108
Pan-Fried Catfish with Capers and
    Cream, 40
Catfish, 34
    Asian Broiled Catfish, 37
    Barbecued Catfish with Pomegranate
      Sauce, 35
    Barbecued Catfish with Thyme, 38
    Mexican Broiled Catfish, 37
    New Orleans Pasta with Catfish, 38
    Pan-Fried Catfish with Capers and
      Cream, 40
    Steamed Catfish with Ginger, 40
    Stir-Fried Spicy Catfish, 35
Cheese, 20
    Blue Cheese-Bacon Dressing, 86
Chilean sea bass, 51
Chiles, 20, 21
    Barbecued Snapper with Maple
      Syrup, Chiles, and Lemon, 71
    Barbecued Swordfish with Chiles and
      Garlic, 91
    Barbecued Trout with Marmalade,
      and Chiles, 94
    Chipotle-Lime Compound Butter, 108
    Chipotle Rub, 99
    Roasted Trout with Raisins, Chiles,
      and Cinammon, 96
Cilantro, mincing, 48
Coconut
    Barbecued Coconut-Pineapple
      Black Cod, 25
    Coconut-Curry Sauce, 48
    Pasta with Grilled Halibut, 48
Coconut Milk, 21
    Salmon Braised in, 65
Cod, 26 *See also* Black Cod
Curries, 48, 77

D, E

Dips, 106, 107, 108
Equipment, essential, 18–19

F

Figs
    Barbecued Trout with Grilled
      Figs, 93
    Broiled Salmon and Figs, 63
Fish
    blackened, 75
    choosing, 10
    cooking techniques, 13–17
    deboning, 18
    determining doneness of, 12
    flouring/battering, 12
    freezing/thawing, 10

marinating, 11
paper-wrapping, 49
prosciutto-wrapped, 52
rinsing, 11
scaling, 18
skinning, 19
smell of, 12
storing, 11
See also specific fish
Fish sauce, 21
Fish screens, 18
Flatfish, 52

G

Garlic
    Barbecued Swordfish with Chiles
      and Garlic, 91
    Lemon-Garlic Rub, 56
    Olive-Garlic Pesto, 94
    pressing, 19
    roasting, 37
    Steamed Halibut with Garlic
      Blanket, 43
Ginger, 21
    Lemon-Ginger Compound
      Butter, 108
    Plank-Smoked Black Cod with Dill
      and Ginger, 31
    Salmon Cakes with Dill and
      Ginger, 65
    shredding, 40
    Steamed Catfish with Ginger, 40
Glazes, 51, 63
Grapefruit
    Barbecued Salmon with
      Grapefruit, 58
    Sauce, Sweet-Sour, 43
Grapes, Broiled Snapper with Peaches
    and, 72
Grouper, 44
Guacamole, 108

H

Halibut, 42
    Barbecued Halibut with Sweet-Sour
      Grapefruit Sauce, 43
    Coconut Pasta with Grilled
      Halibut, 48
    Greek Roasted Halibut, 46
    Pan-Fried Halibut with Herbs, Olive
      Oil, and Soy, 49
    Pan-Roasted Halibut with
      Apricots, 44
    Paper-Wrapped Halibut, 49

    Poached Halibut with Spicy Orange
      Sauce, 51
    Roasted Halibut with Fruit Glaze, 51
    Roasted in Prosciutto, 52
    Steamed Halibut with Garlic
      Blanket, 43
    Stir-Fried Orange-Hoisin Halibut, 46
    Tex-Mex Barbecued Halibut
      Steaks, 48
    Thai Plank-Smoked Halibut, 44
Herbs, 21
Hoisin sauce, 21
Honey-Lime Salad Dressing, 32

I, K

Ingredients, essential, 20–23
Ketchup, Spicy, 83, 108

L

Lemons
    Barbecued Snapper with Maple
      Syrup, Chiles, and Lemon, 71
    Broiled Lemon Sole with
      Mushrooms, 83
    Lemon-Dill Mayonnaise, 29
    Lemon Dry Rub, 60
    Lemon-Garlic Rub, 56
    Lemon-Ginger Compound Butter, 108
    Sauce, 77
    Sauce, Spicy, 93
    Tomato-Lemon Sauce, 81
Limes
    Barbecued Lemon Sole with Apricot
      and Lime, 79
    Chipotle-Lime Compound Butter, 108
    Honey-Lime Salad Dressing, 32
Lingcod, 64

M

Mahi mahi, 102
Mango Salsa, 107
Maple Syrup, Barbecued Snapper with
    Chiles, Lemon, and, 71
Marmalade, Barbecued Trout with
    Chiles and, 94
Microwaving, 17
Mint-Basil Compound Butter, 108
Monkfish, 66
Mushrooms
    Broiled Lemon Sole with
      Mushrooms, 83
    Pan-Fried Snapper with Shiitake
      Cream Sauce, 72

O

Oils, 21, 22
Olives, 22
    Greek Roasted Halibut, 46
    Olive-Garlic Pesto, 94
    Pan-Fried Black Cod with Tomatoes
        and Olives, 25
    pitting, 19
    tapenade, 22
Ono, 104
Opah, 88
Orange roughy, 79
Oranges
    Spicy Orange Sauce, 51
    Stir-Fried Orange-Hoisin Halibut, 46
Oyster sauce, 22

P

Pan-frying, 15
Papaya, Salmon, and Avocado Salad, 61
paper-wrapping, 49
Pasta
    Coconut Pasta with Grilled
        Halibut, 48
    New Orleans Pasta with Catfish, 38
    Salmon Pasta Salad, 56
    Swordfish-Mushroom Pasta, 89
Peaches, Broiled Snapper with Grapes
    and, 72
Peppers, roasted, 22
Pestos, 71, 94
Pike, 74
Pineapple-Coconut Black Cod,
    Barbecued, 25
Pine Nut-Crusted Black Cod, 26
Plank cooking, 31
Poaching, 16
Pomegranate molasses/syrup, 22
Pomegranate Sauce, 35
Pompano, 96
Potato-Crusted Sole with Spicy
    Ketchup, 83
Prosciutto, wrapping fish with, 52

R

Raisins, Chiles and Cinnamon, Roasted
    Trout with, 96
Roasting, 15
Rockfish, 32
Rubs, 26, 56, 60, 99

S

Sablefish. *See* Black Cod
Salads
    Asian Grilled Salmon Salad, 64
    Caesar Salad with Grilled Tuna, 101

Grilled Swordfish Salad with Blue
    Cheese-Bacon Dressing, 86
Salmon, Papaya, and Avocado
    Salad, 61
Salmon Pasta Salad, 56
Seared Tuna Salad, 99
Salmon, 54–55
    Asian Grilled Salmon Salad, 64
    Barbecued Salmon Skewers, 58
    Barbecued Salmon with
        Grapefruit, 58
    Barbecued Salmon with Lemon-
        Garlic Rub, 56
    Braised in Coconut Milk, 65
    Broiled Salmon and Figs, 63
    Broiled Salmon with Teriyaki-Butter
        Glaze, 63
    Cakes with Dill and Ginger, 65
    Chilled Salmon with Jade Sauce, 68
    environmental concerns about, 61
    Pasta Salad, 56
    removing pin bones from, 56
    removing skin from, 61
    Roasted Salmon with Herb
        Mayonnaise, 68
    Salmon, Papaya, and Avocado
        Salad, 61
    Smoked Salmon with Lemon Dry
        Rub, 60
    Stir-Fried Salmon with Asparagus, 60
    Tea-Poached Salmon with Mint, 64
    Thai Steamed Salmon, 66
Salsas, 28, 32, 85, 106–7
Sauces, 106–8
    Aioli Dipping Sauce, 107
    Caper-Dill Sauce, 108
    Coconut-Curry Sauce, 48
    Jade Sauce, 68, 106
    Lemon Sauce, 77
    New Wave Tartar Sauce, 107
    Pomegranate Sauce, 35
    Shiitake Cream Sauce, 72
    Spicy Lemon Sauce, 93
    Spicy Orange Sauce, 51
    Spicy Wasabi Sauce, 107
    Sweet-Sour Grapefruit Sauce, 43
    Tartar Sauce, 107
    Tomato-Lemon Sauce, 81
    Wasabi Sauce, 104
Sausage
    New Orleans Pasta with Catfish, 38
    Pan-Roasted Black Cod with
        Andouille Sausage, 28
Sesame seeds, 22, 68
Shark, 89
Sherry, dry, 23

Snapper
    about, 70
    Barbecued Snapper with Maple Syrup,
        Chiles, and Lemon, 71
    Broiled Snapper with Peaches and
        Grapes, 72
    Green Thai–Curried Snapper, 77
    New Orleans-Style Blackened
        Snapper, 75
    Pan-Fried Snapper with Lemon
        Sauce, 77
    Pan-Fried Snapper with Shiitake
        Cream Sauce, 72
    Pan-Fried Tangerine Snapper, 75
    Steamed Snapper with Spicy
        Pesto, 71
    Stove-Top Smoked Snapper, 74
Sole, 78
    Barbecued Lemon Sole with Apricot
        and Lime, 79
    Broiled Lemon Sole with
        Mushrooms, 83
    Pan-Fried Sole with Brown Butter, 82
    Pan-Fried Sole with Toasted
        Almonds, 82
    Pan-Fried Sole with Tomato-Lemon
        Sauce, 81
    Pan-Fried Sole with Wilted
        Spinach, 81
    petrale, cooking, 82
    Potato-Crusted Sole with Spicy
        Ketchup, 83
Soy sauce, 23
Spinach, Wilted, Pan-Fried Sole
    with, 81
Steaming, 17
Stir-frying, 16
Stove-top smokers, 74
Sturgeon, 86
Swordfish, 84
    Barbecued Swordfish with Chiles
        and Garlic, 91
    Broiled Swordfish with Compound
        Butters, 89
    Cantonese Stir-fried Swordfish, 85
    Chinese Barbecued Swordfish, 88
    Grilled Swordfish Salad with Blue
        Cheese-Bacon Dressing, 86
    grilling, 91
    Pan-Roasted Swordfish with
        Caramelized Onions, 88
    Swordfish-Mushroom Pasta, 89
    Tacos with Mango Salsa, 85
    trimming bloodline from, 85

T

Tangerine Snapper, Pan-Fried, 75
Tartar sauces, 107
Tea-Poached Salmon with Mint, 64
Tilapia, 72
Tomatoes, 23
    Mexican Salsa, 107
    Pan-Fried Black Cod with Tomatoes
        and Olives, 25
    Tomato-Lemon Sauce, 81
Tortillas
    Swordfish Tacos with Mango
        Salsa, 85
    Wok-Seared Tuna in Flour
        Tortillas, 102
Tostados, Barbecued Black Cod, 32
Trout, 92
    Barbecued Trout with Grilled
        Figs, 93
    Barbecued Trout with Marmalade,
        and Chiles, 94
    Braised Trout with Olive-Garlic
        Pesto, 94
    Pan-Fried Trout Fillets, 96
    Pan-Fried Trout in Spicy Lemon
        Sauce, 93
    Roasted Trout with Raisins, Chiles,
        and Cinammon, 96
Tuna, 98
    Asian Grilled Tuna, 102
    Caesar Salad with Grilled Tuna, 101
    cutting, 101
    Grilled Peppered Tuna, 101
    Grilled Tuna Skewers with Chipotle
        Rub, 99
    Seared Tuna Burger with Wasabi
        Sauce, 104
    Seared Tuna Salad, 99
    Spicy Tuna Cakes, 104

V, W, Z

Vinegars, 23
Walleyed pike, 74
Wasabi, 23
    sauces, 104, 107
Wood chips, 23
Zucchini matchsticks, 46

Other Cookbooks by
Hugh Carpenter & Teri Sandison

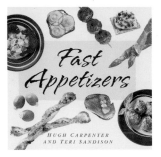

A flavorful collection of quick and easy entrées, perfect for work-night cooking. The book for everyone who's ever complained that they just don't have the time to cook.

With their emphasis on short ingredients lists and plenty of make-ahead tips, the 100 recipes in *Wok Fast* are tailored to accommodate tight schedules, without sacrificing flavor.

More than 100 recipes, from spring rolls to pizza to caviar, that can be made in a flash, most in under 15 minutes. Whether you're hosting a cocktail party or an intimate dinner, these dishes deliver maximum flavor in minimum time.

Platters of tender, juicy ribs have long reigned as home-cooking favorites. *The Great Ribs Book* brings you the lowdown on the different types of ribs, cooking techniques, sauces, and more. Includes more than sixty recipes pairing ribs with delectable flavors from all over the world.

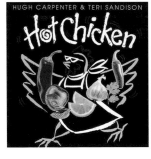

Fifty bold and sophisticated yet easy stir-fry recipes seasoned with a host of exciting ingredients. Perfect ideas for fresh, healthy weeknight meals or weekend entertaining. Includes more than fifty vibrant color photos.

Fifty wild and zesty recipes that combine chicken with the distinct flavors and cuisines of the world. Discover delicious and elegant ways to serve one of the most versatile and healthful meats. More than fifty color photos provide dramatic presentation ideas.

More of the winning Hot formula: sixty-plus original recipes, organized alphabetically from artichokes to zucchini, introduce a palate-tingling world of veggie-based soups, salads, pastas, sides, and entrées.

Fifty fresh and sensational recipes take pasta to new and dazzling heights. Packed with easy, inventive ideas, this is the complete resource for busy cooks at all levels of experience. Includes more than fifty exciting color photos.

Fifty sizzling recipes for classic barbecue favorites and innovative pleasers from around the world. From simple any-night delights to elaborate weekend feasts, this tantalizing offering will heat up backyards and kitchens alike.